All About
Roses

—⟲—

Created and designed by
the editorial staff of
ORTHO BOOKS

Endorsed by the
American Rose Society

Project Editor
Ken Burke

Writers
Rex Wolf & James McNair

Designers
Barbara Ziller & John Williams

Illustrators
Carla Simmons & Ron Hildebrand

Ortho Books

Publisher
Robert L. Iacopi

Editorial Director
Min S. Yee

Managing Editors
Anne Coolman
Michael D. Smith
Sally W. Smith

Production Director
Ernie S. Tasaki

Editors
Richard H. Bond
Alice E. Mace

System Consultant
Mark Zielinski

Asst. System Managers
Linda Bouchard
William F. Yusavage

Photographic Director
Alan Copeland

Photographers
Laurie A. Black
Richard A. Christman

Asst. Production Manager
Darcie S. Furlan

Associate Editor
Jill Fox

Production Editors
Deborah Cowder
Anne Pederson

Chief Copy Editor
Rebecca Pepper

Photo Editors
Kate O'Keeffe
Pam Peirce
Raymond F. Quinton

National Sales Manager
Charles H. Aydelotte

Sales Associate
Susan B. Boyle

Operations Assistant
Gail L. Davis

Administrative Assistant
Georgiann Wright

Address all inquiries to
Ortho Books
Chevron Chemical Company
Consumer Products Division
575 Market Street
San Francisco, CA 94105

Chevron Chemical Company
575 Market Street, San Francisco, CA 94105

Front Cover Photo: 'Queen Elizabeth'

Back Cover Photos: Top left: Climbing polyantha rose. Top right: 'Ivory Fashion'. Bottom left: 'Double Delight'. Bottom right: 'Angel Face'.

Title Page: 'Chicago Peace'.

Acknowledgments:

Encyclopedia of Roses
compiled by Mark S. Frappier

**Special consultant,
rose identification and photography:**
Douglas Rhymes, Filoli Rosarian

Special thanks to:

The American Rose Society for reviewing and correcting the manuscript

Academy of Sciences
Golden Gate Park, San Francisco, CA

Don and Becky Herzog
Miniature Plant Kingdom

Tom Liggett
Liggett's Rose Nursery

George Rose
All America Rose Selection

Stocking Rose Nursery
San Jose, CA

Miriam Wilkins
Heritage Rose Society

Barbara Worl
Sweetbriar Press

Typography by CBM Type
Sunnyvale, CA

Color separations by Color Tech
Redwood City, CA

Copy editing by Judith Chaffin

Production editing by Jessie Wood

Proofreading and indexing by editcetera
Berkeley, CA

Photography:
(Names of photographers in alphabetical order are followed by page numbers on which their work appears. R = right, C = center, L = left, B = bottom.)

Armstrong Nurseries: 81C

Martha Baker: 47, 88TL, Back cover TL

Laurie A. Black: 17, 32, 33, 36, 74TC

Derek Fell: 5, 7TL, 7TR, 7C, 16B, 26, 60, 63TL, 67C, 71BL, 74BC, 75TL, 75CB, 76TL, 77C, 77BR, 78C, 78TR, 79CL, 79BL, 79C, 83TR, 84C, 86C 86TR, 87BR, 88TC, 90, 91, 92R, Back cover TR, BL

Barbara Ferguson: 79R

Charles Marden Fitch: 86BR, 87L

Pamela Harper: 10, 11T, 18, 24T, 61, 62TC, 62BC, 63BL, 63BR, 64TR, 64BR, 65TL, 65TR, 65BR, 66L, 66BR, 67TL, 68TL, 68C, 68TR, 69C, 69R, 80R, 83BR, 85C, 85BR, 87C, 87TR, 92L

Jackson and Perkins: 50, 51

Susan Lammers: Front cover, 79R, 82TL, 84R

Michael Lamotte and Sara Slavin: 53, 54, 55, 56, 57, 58, 59

Michael McKinley: 8BR, 9BL, 9BR, 19, 20, 21L, 24B, 25TL, 63TR, 64BL, Back cover BR

James McNair: 27

Muriel and Arthur Norman Orans: 4, 7BC, 14R, 20TL, 22B, 28, 29, 37, 62TR, 64TL, 65BL, 70C, 71TL, 71C, 71TL, 71C, 72BL, 73C, 73R, 76BL, 78L, 80CL, 81TL, 82BL, 83TL, 84TL, 84BL, 88BR

Ortho Books: 25BR, 30, 40B, 77L, 88TR

Ann Reilly: 1, 12B, 16TR, 22T, 25BL, 36B, 40T, 62TL, 66TL, 70BL, 70TR, 72TL, 72C, 74BL, 76C, 76R, 78BR, 80C, 81R, 82C, 82R, 89

Douglas Rhymes: 7BL, 11B, 12T, 13, 65C, 66BL, 66TR, 67BL, 67R, 68BL, 68BR, 69TL, 69BL, 70TL, 71R, 72BL, 72TR, 73B, 74TL, 74R, 75BL, 75CT, 75R, 79TL, 80BL, 83BL, 85L, 85TR, 86L, 88BL

Joe Schopplein: 6T, 6B

George Taloumis: 7BR, 14L, 15TL, 21R, 62BR, 70BR, 73TR, 77TR, 81BL

All About Roses

1

THE HISTORY AND DEVELOPMENT OF THE ROSE

From heritage roses to modern hybrids, this chapter is a guide to understanding rose terminology and classifications.

2

ROSES IN THE LANDSCAPE

Roses don't belong only in formal gardens. Here's information on landscaping and designing with roses in all of their varied forms.

3

PLANTING AND CARE

The basics of rose culture and maintenance: choosing healthy plants, and how to plant them; watering; mulching; fertilizing; protection from pests; pruning; propagating; and more.

4

ENJOYING ROSES INDOORS

In this chapter you'll find instructions on how to cut and arrange roses for long life and beauty, and recipes for making your own potpourri.

5

ENCYCLOPEDIA OF ROSES

Here's the information you need to help you decide which of the hundreds of available varieties of species roses, shrub roses, old garden roses, hybrid teas, floribundas, polyanthas, grandifloras, climbers, and miniatures are right for your garden.

The History and Development of the Rose

ROSES HAVE BEEN CULTIVATED
FOR CENTURIES IN MANY LANDS.
TODAY'S GARDENER CAN CHOOSE
FROM A WIDE SELECTION, FROM
OLD FAVORITES TO NEW EXAMPLES
OF THE HYBRIDIZER'S ART.

The rose is often proclaimed "Queen of the Flowers" by gardeners, and there are few flowers that can make a better claim to the title. Roses are grown primarily for the beauty and fragrance of their flowers, which can be found in an astonishing array of shapes and sizes and in almost every color of the spectrum. Roses have been tended and enjoyed by generations of modern-day gardeners, and their lineage under cultivation stretches back many hundreds of years.

Species of the genus *Rosa* have been identified almost everywhere in the Northern Hemisphere, as far north as Alaska and Norway and as far south as North Africa and Mexico. Fossilized plants over 30 million years old can be linked to modern rose species.

The Chinese were probably the first to cultivate roses. Five hundred years before the birth of Christ, Confucius wrote of the roses in the Imperial Gardens. Roses had been under cultivation in China for over 2,000 years before Chinese roses were introduced to the European market in the late eighteenth century.

The seedbed of European rose growing was in the Middle East, in Persia and Mesopotamia, but little is known about the types of roses grown in those countries, or the methods of their cultivation. The ancient Persians established a flourishing trade in precious attar of roses, a fragrant oil distilled from rose petals, so they must have been adept at rose cultivation.

The ancient Greeks cultivated roses extensively—for the beauty of the flowers, for medicinal purposes, and as a perfume. The rose was dedicated to two deities: Aphrodite, the goddess of love and beauty; and Dionysus, the god of revelry. Wreaths and garlands of roses were prominently featured at festivals in their honor.

It was during the peak years of the Roman Empire (the first three centuries after the birth of Christ) that rose cultivation reached its peak in the ancient world. The Romans imported roses from Egypt. They also established a thriving rose-growing industry at Paestum, south of Rome. Methods were developed to force roses into bloom during winter by growing them in greenhouses or by irrigating plants with warm water. Private rose gardens were universal for the nobility and the rich, and large public rose gardens were frequented and enjoyed by the populace.

The poet Horace half-jokingly expressed concern that the amount of land devoted to roses might produce a shortage of grain. Typically excessive, the emperor Nero spent vast sums of money to cover his guests with rose petals, which he arranged to have fall from the ceiling. During the first century A.D., Pliny the Elder described several different species of roses in his *Natural History*.

Left: Hybrid tea 'Color Magic', the 1978 All-America Rose Selection, sports magnificent double blooms.
Above: Hardy Rosa rugosa perfumes the air with its profusion of flowers.

After the fall of the Roman Empire and the demise of Roman culture, the rose fell into disfavor and was grown primarily in monastery gardens for its medicinal value. Roses were thought to be effective in treating a wide variety of ailments. The decorative qualities of roses could not remain ignored for long, however, and after 1000 A.D. the plants began to appear in the manor gardens of the nobility. During the twelfth and thirteenth centuries, warriors returning from the Crusades in the Middle East brought back tales of extensive and splendid rose gardens as well as sample plants. Interest in and cultivation of roses began anew in Europe.

The 30 years of strife in England during the fifteenth century known as the War of the Roses was not named thus because it was fought over roses; rather, it got its name because the two families fighting over the throne of England, the House of York and the House of Lancaster, took the white rose and red rose, respectively, as their symbol. Henry VII united the two families by marriage, and created the symbol of the Tudor rose, a white rose superimposed on a red, which is still the symbol of English royalty.

Came the flowering of the Renaissance with its emphasis on beauty and design, and roses again found favor in both private and public gardens. The expansion of commerce that was part of this period allowed the exchange of different varieties of roses throughout Europe and, later on, its colonial outposts in the New World.

Two important sets of circumstances that occurred in the late eighteenth century led to the explosion of popularity of roses that continues unabated to this day. The first was the introduction to the West of roses from China in 1752. Just about every modern rose can trace its ancestry to one of the roses imported from China. The second boost to the popularity of roses was given by the empress Josephine of France. After she married Napoleon in 1796 she set about creating a garden at the Chateau Malmaison on the outskirts of Paris that contained exotic plants from all over the world. She became particularly intrigued with roses and set out to collect and plant at Malmaison all known varieties. Competition was fierce among the rose growers of the continent and England, but her patronage gave special impetus to French breeders, who dominated the market until well into the twentieth century.

At the time of the empress's death in 1814 her garden at Malmaison contained over 250 varieties, and collecting and growing roses had become a popular pastime for the fashionable set and the new merchant class alike. A further legacy of the empress Josephine was the encouragement she gave her drawing master, Pierre Joseph Redouté, to take up botanical illustration. Redouté showed great talent with exquisitely rendered watercolors.

His best-known work is *Les Roses*, completed in 1824. It features 167 color plates of roses from all over the world from the classical period, the Middle Ages, and the early nineteenth century. Few illustrators since have approached his ability to render anatomical details accurately while at the same time capturing the beauty of the rose's color and form in an almost magical way.

Two illustrations from Redouté's 1824 masterpiece, Les Roses, *give us a glimpse of early rose varieties.*

SPECIES, HYBRIDS, AND SPORTS

In the genus *Rosa* there are over 150 *species*, or types of roses that have specific characteristics. These *species roses* are plants that grow in the wild and from which all other roses are descended. Two different roses can combine very easily to produce a rose that has some of the characteristics of both parents but an identity of its own. In this process, known as *hybridization*, pollen from one plant fertilizes the ovary of another. Plants grown from the resulting seed will be *hybrids*. Hybridization frequently happens in nature, with bees and other insects being the carriers of the pollen, but the process has been developed to an intricate art by modern hybridizers. Because of their efforts, there are now more than one thousand different kinds of roses. The different versions of a species are called *varieties*. The varieties developed by hybridizers are called *cultivars*. (See pages 15–16 for a discussion of modern rose hybridizers, and pages 50–51 for instruction on how roses are cross-pollinated.)

Varieties and cultivars may also be the result of a sport rather than hybridization. A *sport* is a chance genetic mutation that occurs in a species. Sports bear a resemblance to the species but often have radically different flowers or growth habits.

CLASSIFICATION OF ROSES

With so many roses to choose from, gardeners need some sort of classification system. They need to be able to differentiate among all these roses in general and specific ways. Let's start by dividing roses into three broad types: species and shrub roses; old garden roses; and modern roses.

Species roses, as discussed above, are those found growing in the wild. *Shrub roses* are close relatives of species roses that have been improved by hybridizers for garden culture. *Old garden roses*, or simply *old roses*, are rose varieties and cultivars clearly identifiable before 1867 with a specific group of roses. This date of 1867 was established by the American Rose Society to commemorate the introduction of what was considered to be the first hybrid tea rose, 'La France', in that year. All rose groups introduced after this date are considered *modern roses*.

Growers produce exquisite colors through hybridization. The elegant hybrid tea 'Double Delight' (directly above) is the result of crossing 'Granada' (top left) and creamy 'Garden Party' (top right).

Introduction of the first hybrid tea rose—'La France'—marked the beginning of the modern roses.

'Chicago Peace', a sport of the hybrid tea 'Peace' at right, is the charming result of a chance genetic mutation.

SPECIES AND SHRUB ROSES

We shall deal with species and shrub roses together because they share many characteristics. The line that divides the two is often very narrow: Shrub roses are usually closely related to specific species; while true, unadulterated species plants are difficult to find, most having been improved on by rose breeders.

There are probably over 150 species of roses in the world, though the exact number is disputable. Roses cross-pollinate so freely and easily that great picking of nits is involved in deciding if a rose is simply another natural hybrid or a new species.

Species and shrub roses require relatively little maintenance. Most are hardy in cold climates, and they require less pruning than modern roses.

Some roses bloom only once during the spring or summer, but many have a second, lesser bloom in the fall. Many have single flowers, that is, a single row of five petals, giving the flowers a simple and delicate appearance that many gardeners appreciate. Many species and shrub roses produce a decorative bonus of colorful and distinctive *hips*, or seed pods, in the fall.

Be sure to allow enough room in your garden for these plants, for some can grow to be 8 feet tall and as wide. Use them as a hedge, or even as a ground cover, or as a magnificent backdrop for other plants.

The following list gives brief descriptions of species and shrub roses you may wish to include in your garden.

Rosa foetida. This plant is a spindly bush, not terribly vigorous, needing a stake or a wall to grow against. It grows to 5–6 feet tall and 4 feet wide. Flowers are single, in a brilliant yellow, with a heavy, unusual fragrance. This species is best known for two sports: *Rosa foetida bicolor*, known as Austrian copper, which has the brilliant yellow of *R. foetida* on the face of the flower but is orange-red on the underside of the petals; and *Rosa foetida persiana* (Persian Yellow), which has luxuriant double yellow flowers. These plants are very susceptible to blackspot, unfortunately, and should not be planted close to other roses in the garden.

Rosa × harisonii (Harison's Yellow). This rose was developed in New York in the early nineteenth century and became naturalized all across the North American continent, spread by settlers moving westward. A vigorous grower to at least 5 feet tall, it produces in spring a profusion of bright yellow, double, fragrant flowers against bright green foliage.

Rosa hugonis (Father Hugo rose). Found by Father Hugh Scallon in China in 1899, this shrub produces semidouble, light-yellow flowers on drooping branches. The flowers have a slight yeasty fragrance. *R. hugonis* grows 6–8 feet tall and almost as wide.

Rosa laevigata (Cherokee rose). A climbing shrub, its blossoms are fragrant, creamy white, and single, 3 inches across with contrasting gold stamens. This plant is not hardy in the far north.

Rosa moyesii. This vigorous shrub can grow as large as 12 feet tall and 10 feet wide. It has an open habit, however, so

plants that like partial shade can be grown with it. Blossoms start in late spring and continue for several weeks. The flowers are 3 inch, blood red, and single, with little scent. A popular hybrid offspring is 'Nevada', with 3½-inch semidouble white flowers, which bloom in amazing profusion in early summer and then repeat sporadically throughout the summer and fall.

Rosa eglanteria or ***R. rubiginosa*** (Sweet briar rose, eglantine). Plant this rose in an upwind corner of your garden someplace out of the way. The shrub quickly becomes a thick mass of canes that is difficult to control, but on moist and warm summer evenings the distinctive scented foliage will prove a delight. The small, pink, single flowers bloom for only a short period of time. 'Lady Penzance' (pink and yellow flowers) and 'Lord Penzance' (yellow flowers) are favorite hybrids.

Rosa rubrifolia. This exceptional plant is grown mainly for the decorative quality of its reddish brown bark and gray-green, slightly iridescent foliage. It grows to 6 feet tall and as wide with an open habit. The small, pink flowers bloom in the early summer.

Right: Golden Rosa foetida persiana *intensifies the red-orange of* Rosa foetida bicolor *in this shrub rose planting.*

Rosa rugosa (Japanese rose, ramanas rose, rugosa rose). Very hardy, this species grows 3–6 feet in height with a spread of 4 feet. Fragrant, single, carmine flowers bloom from spring to fall, followed by the appearance of large, brilliant, red hips rich in vitamin C. The crinkled leaves are a shiny dark green. There are many fine hybrids with flowers in varying shades of pink, white, and red. Rugosas will grow in almost any soil and are particularly good near the seashore, since they are not affected by ocean spray. The plants can be trained into a good hedge.

Rosa spinosissima (Scotch or burnet rose). This species is low-growing (under 3 feet) but spreads rapidly by means of suckers, making it a good ground cover. The single flowers are 1½ inches wide and fragrant. Distinctive, almost black hips adorn the plant in the fall.

Wilhelm Kordes, a famous German rose breeder, used *R. spinosissima* to create a spectacular succession of cultivars called the Frühlings series. 'Frühlingsgold' has huge, golden-yellow, semidouble flowers 3½–5 inches across. Mature plants are much larger than the *R. spinosissima* parent, growing 6–8 feet tall and almost as wide.

Rosa virginiana. Another native to North America, this large (6 feet high by 5 feet wide) shrub bears its pink single flowers in midsummer on long, arching canes. It suckers vigorously, so confine it to a bed and keep the suckers cut back unless you want it to spread. 'Plena', with double pink flowers and a slightly more compact habit, is a favorite hybrid.

Rosa wichuraiana (Memorial rose). This native of East Asia is a low-growing, spreading plant perfect for use as a ground cover on a slope. The stems root where they touch the ground. Single and semidouble, slightly fragrant clusters of white flowers bloom in late summer above lush green foliage. The hybrid 'Hiawatha' has red flowers with the same growth habits. Climbing hybrids include 'Blaze', 'Dr. W. Van Fleet', and 'New Dawn'.

Below: The large, ruffly blossoms of Rosa moyesii *'Nevada', a prolific bloomer, make this vigorously growing shrub rose an ideal choice for an impressive display planting. Its large white blossoms may be splashed with red.*

OLD GARDEN ROSES

For over half a century, the so-called old garden roses have been out of favor with the rose-buying public, the spotlight being dominated by hybrid tea roses and other groups developed within the last hundred years. But recently there has been renewed interest in these old-fashioned roses, and a greater and greater number of cultivars is becoming commercially available. This renaissance may stem from a nostalgia for the past. It may have come about simply because some gardeners desire the attributes of powerful fragrance, disease resistance, and hardiness that many old roses possess, or simply because they enjoy the different flower forms of these roses. Whatever the case, rose fanciers find it a welcome development to have available a full range of choices of forms of these remarkable flowers.

As we mentioned earlier, old roses are those groups introduced before 1867, when the first hybrid tea rose, 'La France', appeared. New varieties in the "old" groups have been introduced since that time; the classification is a somewhat arbitrary device that recognizes the great popularity that hybrid teas enjoyed after their introduction. The following are the major groups of old roses in roughly the same order that they were introduced.

Gallica. Records show that the *Rosa gallica*, or French rose, was under cultivation in the sixteenth century. It is the earliest European species still extant. *Rosa gallica officinalis*, called the apothecary rose, was grown during the Middle Ages in almost every monastery garden for use in a variety of herbal remedies.

Gallica plants form compact bushes 3–4 feet high. Be careful if your gallica is growing on its own roots (that is, if it has not been grafted); it spreads easily by means of runners if not kept under control. This rose is quite hardy and will tolerate poor soil. The fragrant flowers bloom once in early summer. The flowers may be single, semidouble, or double, in shades of deep red through purple to pink. Some varieties are marbled or striped with white.

Damask. The ancestors of Damask roses were native to the eastern Mediterranean and were probably introduced to western Europe by Crusaders returning from their wars. The plants are 3–7 feet tall and are hardy, but they require good soil. Their growth can be rangy, with arching canes that will have to be staked if the blossoms are to be fully appreciated. The summer damask (*Rosa damascena*) blooms once in midsummer; the autumn damask (*Rosa damascena semperflorens*) usually has a second bloom in the fall. Medium-size double or semidouble flowers grow in large clusters in shades of pink. The flowers are particularly valued for their fragrance.

Alba. The white rose of York (*Rosa alba*) is of uncertain parentage, but it was probably the white rose grown by the Romans, who introduced it as far north as England. It became very popular during the Renaissance, and it is often seen in Italian paintings of the period. The plant is quite hardy and both pest- and disease-resistant, growing densely 6–9 feet high with distinctive gray-green foliage. It blooms once annually in late spring or early summer. The flowers are of medium size, usually semidouble, delicate, and fragrant, in shades of pink as well as white.

Centifolia. The huge, very fragrant flowers of *Rosa centifolia* (literally "hundred-leaved") are familiar to many gardeners as the cabbage rose. Of uncertain, diverse parentage, *R. centifolia* was first produced by Dutch hybridizers in the sixteenth century. Ranging in height from 3½ feet to 7 feet, the long canes need staking or other support if the flowers are to be properly appreciated. Most plants are quite susceptible to mildew; quickly take corrective action (see page 43) if you notice mildew growth.

The very double, 2½–5-inch blossoms appear in clusters once a year in late spring or early summer. Flowers range in color from shades of reddish purple to pink, often with darker centers.

Moss. Moss roses, sports of the centifolia, made their debut in the late seventeenth century. They are similar to their parent in growth habit and flowers, but their primary

characteristic is a green or reddish brown mosslike covering on the flower stems and sepals that is fragrant and sticky to the touch. The plants are quite hardy but enjoy being well cultivated.

Most varieties bloom only once, in early summer, in shades of white, pink, crimson, or reddish purple.

China. The introduction to the West in 1752 of the first China rose (*Rosa chinensis*) was a significant milestone in the history of rose breeding. The China roses were *remontant*, or repeat bloomers, flowering in early summer and again in the fall, a great advantage when compared to most of the Western roses, which, with the exception of the autumn damask, have only one relatively short blooming period a year.

Most Chinas are medium-size plants with an open and airy growth habit, good-looking as bedding plants or in containers. They are tender plants that prefer a moist soil. Flowers are small and grow in clusters in shades of pink, red, and crimson, with little fragrance.

Breeders were not immediately successful in producing crosses between the "new" China rose and European species. In fact, the first cross was a natural one discovered on the Ile de Bourbon (now Reunion Island) in the Indian Ocean. 'Old Blush' combined with an autumn damask rose to produce what came to be known as Bourbon roses.

Bourbon. These roses became one of the most popular groups of roses in the early nineteenth century. The plants are vigorous growers, some reaching 6 feet, and often need some sort of support. They are generally tender. Their main blooming period is in midsummer, but most bloom again in the autumn. Bourbon roses differ from their predecessors in that they produce blooms on new wood that has grown the same season. Flower forms are usually semidouble or double, in shades of white, pink, red, and purple, with a slight applelike scent.

Portland. Portland roses resulted from a cross between another China rose, 'Slater's Crimson China', and the autumn damask. These cultivars are very like the Bourbon roses, but they have stronger colors and generally smaller flowers. They never achieved the great popularity of the Bourbons.

Tea. Another import from China, the tea rose (*Rosa × odorata*) was introduced in the West in 1808. Closely related to the China rose, tea roses are distinguished by their distinctive tealike fragrance and larger, fuller flowers. The teas also bloom through the summer into the fall and are, unfortunately, quite tender. Blossoms are semidouble or double in shades of white, pink, and yellow.

Noisette. The first hybrid rose group to originate in North America was the noisette, introduced in 1818. A cross between the China rose and the musk rose (*Rosa moschata*), noisettes are climbers, growing up to 20 feet. They are not hardy in the north. Blooms appear throughout the summer and fall in clusters of white, pink, yellow, or red flowers with a fragrance like that of the tea rose.

Hybrid Perpetual. The hybrid perpetual group of roses is the precursor of the modern rose. It would be impossible to determine exactly the parentage of these roses; they probably resulted from repeated crossings of noisettes, teas, Portlands, and Bourbons. Hybrid perpetuals became immensely popular during the last half of the 1800s, when over 4,000 varieties were introduced.

Their popularity was well deserved. Hybrid perpetuals are hardy, vigorous plants producing large (up to 7 inches), mostly double flowers. "Perpetual" is, however, a bit of an overstatement: There is a profuse bloom in early summer, then a rest of a few weeks, and (usually) a second bloom in the fall. The quality and quantity of the fall flowers can vary from year to year. The fragrant blooms are usually solid colors ranging from white to pink to maroon.

A selection of old garden roses, all in cultivation by the early nineteenth century. Opposite: Rosa gallica versicolor. Above: Alba rose 'Königin von Dänemark'. Left: A repeat-blooming China rose, 'Old Blush'.

MODERN ROSES

The groups of roses classified as modern roses are those that were introduced after 1867. Nearly all the roses you find in your local nursery or garden center will be modern roses, as will most of those offered by mail-order (except for specialty) suppliers.

The large number of hybridized cultivars and the sophisticated techniques used by plant breeders have resulted in a stunning array of roses in colors, flower forms, number of blooms, and growth habits. There is a modern rose to delight any gardener. Let's look at the five main groups of modern roses: the hybrid teas, polyanthas, floribundas, grandifloras, and the miniatures.

Hybrid tea. Hybrid tea roses are the most widely grown roses in the world today. It is, of course, the beauty of the

Above: Hybrid tea 'Duet', an All-America Rose Selection.
Below: Clustered blooms of the polyantha 'China Doll'.

blossoms in the fashion of the time that makes them such favorites. Long, narrow buds open into delicate blossoms on straight, tensile stems. Modern hybrid teas are the result of many decades of breeding and interbreeding between hybrid perpetuals and tea roses, and they have gained in hardiness and vigor of growth from the former and fragrance and delicacy of form from the latter.

In 1900 the breeder Joseph Pernet-Ducher introduced 'Soleil d'Or', a second-generation offspring of a form of *Rosa foetida* and a hybrid perpetual. This was the first yellow hybrid tea, and its introduction opened up a whole new range of colors for hybridizers. For a number of years these brightly colored roses were known as Pernetianas, but they were absorbed into the hybrid tea class by the 1930s.

Blooming prolifically from early summer until the first frost, the flowers are borne singly on long stems. Usually double and fragrant, flower colors range from whites through lavenders, pinks, yellows, oranges, and reds, with mixtures and blends between.

Hybrid teas can survive winters without protection in areas where the average minimum winter temperatures are greater than 10°F. Bushes usually grow to heights of 2½–3½ feet, though some varieties, if left unmolested, will reach 6 feet.

Polyantha. The late nineteenth century saw the introduction of the polyantha, a cross between the Oriental *Rosa multiflora* and hybrid teas. These low-growing (up to 2 feet) plants are ideal candidates for mass plantings and low hedges. "Polyantha" is derived from the Greek word for "many flowered," and these roses live up to their name, producing a great quantity of small flowers in clusters from late spring through the fall. Polyanthas are much hardier than hybrid teas, and their finely textured, narrow leaves show the parentage of *R. multiflora*. Flowers are single, semidouble, or double, sometimes scented, in white, red, and pastel shades of pink, yellow, and orange. The popularity of polyanthas has been eclipsed in recent years by their more spectacular progeny, the floribunda roses.

Floribunda. Floribundas combine the best qualities of their two parents: From the hybrid teas come the flower form, medium size of flowers, and the foliage; from the polyanthas come the increased hardiness over the hybrid teas, low-growing habit (2–3 feet), and exuberant, continuous bloom from late spring through autumn. The flowers are borne in clusters on stems of medium length. Many cultivars feature fragrant flowers. The many cultivars available cover the entire color range of the hybrid teas.

Grandiflora. Barely more than 30 years old, this group of roses is the result of crosses made between hybrid tea and floribunda roses, again exploiting the best qualities of both parents. The flower form and long stems are carried from the hybrid teas, and the increased hardiness and abundance of continuously blooming flowers are legacies of the floribunda. The flower size is midway between that of the two parents, and flowers are borne either singly or in small clusters. The size of the grandiflora plants, however, bests both the parents: Plants may grow to 3–6 feet or more and are ideal for making a background border that is grand indeed. The blooms are usually double, without a striking fragrance, in solid colors of red, white, pink, orange, and yellow, as well as blends and dramatic bicolors.

TREE ROSES

Tree roses, sometimes called standard roses, are not a class of roses in themselves, but they are considered a distinct garden form. Almost any hybrid tea, floribunda, grandiflora, or miniature rose can be made into a tree rose. Plant growers graft the selected cultivar onto a tall, sturdy trunk of established rootstock to create this elegant form. The flower and foliage characteristics of the grafted plant remain the same.

Standards lend themselves to a variety of landscape uses, particularly in a formal or traditional garden design. They usually need careful pruning (see page 49) to keep their shape symmetrical, round, and full. Special protection against freezing (see page 45) is also necessary, except in mild winter climates.

Flowers of 'White Masterpiece' standard seem more brilliant above 'Janna' (left) and 'Over the Rainbow' miniatures.

MINIATURE ROSES

Thanks to miniature roses, anyone can find room for roses, whether it be indoors or out. Miniature roses, or minis, as they are popularly called, grow 6–18 inches tall, with most averaging about 12 inches. The blooms of these delightful small plants are proportionately small, ranging from a tiny ½ inch wide to 1½ inches wide, while retaining perfect rose flower forms.

The antecedents of miniature roses are vague, but they are probably derived from a Chinese native, *Rosa chinensis minima*, which was introduced in the West in the early 1900s. Miniature roses achieved a certain popularity at this time, when they were known as fairy flowers, but they disappeared from fashion. Interest in them was rekindled in the 1920s, when tiny plants were discovered growing in a window box in a Swiss village. These were propagated and hybridized. Today there are hundreds of different varieties of miniature roses in climbing form, as standards, with flowers in most colors and forms, even including moss roses.

Their compact size makes minis ideal for edgings in beds or as container plants that can be easily moved. They are quite frost hardy outside but can easily be protected in severe climates by moving or covering them. Minis can even be grown indoors under artificial light (see page 53 for their requirements).

CLIMBING ROSES

Climbing roses have been used for centuries to cover walls, trellises, pergolas, and walkways. They bring the beauty and fragrance of the rose to eye and nose level, flooding the senses. Climbing roses are divided into two groups: the large-flowered climbers, which have rigid, thick canes; and the ramblers, which have thinner, flexible canes.

Large-flowered climbers. These plants do not strictly climb, since they have no tendrils or other means to secure support; most climbers are tall plants that need to be loosely secured to some support. Some climbers, however, have canes that are rigid and strong enough to stand on their own to heights of 10 feet, but they are traditionally tied to a pillar or post to prevent them from snapping off in high winds. This subgroup is known as pillar roses.

Large-flowered climbers take about two growing seasons before they become established and start blooming. The plants should not be pruned during these first two years. (See page 48 for instructions on pruning climbing roses.)

Large-flowered climbers produce canes 10–15 feet tall that carry the flowers in clusters. They are relatively hardy and somewhat resistant to disease. The blossoms can be 2–6 inches across in a wide range of flower forms and colors. Most bloom twice, in the early summer and again in the autumn.

Above: Minis form a striking two-toned border, with the intense 'Scarlet Gem' setting off the lighter 'Starina'.

There are climbing versions of hybrid tea roses and their descendants and of polyanthas and miniatures. These are sports: The flowers and foliage resemble the original, but they are often less hardy and bear fewer blooms.

Ramblers. Ramblers have very long (10–20 feet), slender canes that bear thick clusters of small (less than 2-inch) flowers. As long as a rambler has something to lean on, it grows with abandon. Ramblers bloom only once a year in late spring or early summer, but the lack of repeat bloom is more than compensated for by a breathtaking profusion of blossoms. These climbers are extremely hardy but tend to be susceptible to mildew if there is inadequate air circulation around the foliage. Blossoms are semidouble or double in red, pale pink, white, and yellow.

A modern class of hybrid climbers and semiclimbers is the *kordesii*, developed by the German breeder Wilhelm Kordes in the 1950s. These plants grow to heights of 6–12 feet, are very hardy, and produce flowers in clusters throughout the summer and fall. 'Dortmund', with 2½–3½-inch, single, red flowers with white centers, is a popular cultivar in this group.

Left: Climber 'Blaze' shows off clustered scarlet blooms.
Below: 'Paul's Scarlet Climber' makes a dazzling display.

THE DEVELOPMENT OF NEW ROSES

As we have seen from our discussion of old and modern roses, the development of new and improved roses has been constant. There is no reason to believe that this quest for new flower colors and forms, continuous blooms, increased hardiness, and disease resistance will abate. But it would be difficult to predict what the favorite rose of the future will be. Fashion, a notoriously fickle arbitrator, plays a large part in the development of new roses. There is also the potential influence of yet untried or even unthought of crosses that may produce hybrids of unexpectedly high quality or beautiful form.

It is likely, however, that radically new roses will be the offspring of crosses made with species roses that have not yet been the subject of experimentation. These crosses will produce new foliage forms, flower forms, colors, cultural requirements, and degrees of disease resistance. Many rosarians and breeders feel that the introduction of new species is an absolute necessity if the rose is to keep its crown as "Queen of the Flowers." The extensive inbreeding among the hybrid teas and their descendants has now reached the point where increasing numbers of plants are delicate and susceptible to disease, instead of fewer and fewer. But dedicated breeders such as Kordes Sohne in Germany and Sam McGredy in New Zealand, who have done extensive work with crosses with *Rosa spinosissima* (the Scotch rose), are developing the basis of what may be the rose of the future.

Let's take a brief look at the process involved in developing a new rose. Up until mid-nineteenth century, hybridizing was a pretty haphazard process. For many years the mistaken belief persisted that a rose inherited its primary characteristics from the seed parent, and the pollen parent had little influence. (It is now known that products of crosses take characteristics without favoritism from both the pollen parent and the seed parent. Which characteristics will be carried and which characteristics will be rejected by the offspring is the gamble inherent in every cross made.) Complete and accurate records were seldom kept, and it is close to impossible to determine the ancestry of most early hybrids.

Modern hybridizers keep careful records and take advantage of current botanical and genetic knowledge. Add to this imagination, persistence, and a large measure of good luck, and you have a rose breeder's qualifications. Most of the roses currently available have been produced by the work of approximately 50 professional hybridizers in about a dozen countries. In the course of developing new cultivars each of these hybridizers cross-pollinates literally thousands of roses per year, yielding tens of thousands of seeds. The number of possible genetic combinations for new roses is immense; the odds have been placed at about 10,000 to 1 against any specific cross-fertilization producing an outstanding new rose.

Developments in roses are not left entirely in the hands of the professionals. These 50 or so professional breeders are joined by numerous amateurs, some of whom beat the odds and are able to produce an award-winning and commercially successful rose. If you'd like to try hybridizing, the step-by-step instructions on pages 50–51 will help you get started.

TESTING

A rose hybridizer must be patient. It may take 10 years or more from development of a plant to its public introduction. Once a successful breeding is completed, the plant is submitted to a rigorous testing program in the test gardens of a commercial rose grower.

A rose company may evaluate the seedlings of as many as 600 different new roses per year. Ninety-five percent of these originate within the company or with professional hybridizers. From this initial cull, 25–30 will be deemed worthy of further observation. Of these, a dozen or so are kept for more trials and may be grown for as long as 5 years. After this, only 4 or 5 will be chosen for public introduction.

Since roses introduced to the public represent a considerable investment in growing space, time, labor, and promotion, the commercial rose nurseries must select those that will do well in the varied and sometimes extreme climates across North America. In addition to their own test gardens, the nurseries rely on test gardens throughout the country to field-test roses.

During these years of testing, flowers as well as other plant characteristics are carefully judged. Flowers are rated on such factors as petal count, form, resistance to rain, color, repeat bloom, and fragrance. Other attributes considered include resistance to disease, hardiness, appearance of foliage, and growth habit.

PLANT PATENTS

Until the passage of the Townsend-Purnell Plant Patent Act in 1930, a hybridizer could invest in the development of a new rose and reap few financial benefits. As soon as a plant was released, it could be immediately propagated by anyone.

The Plant Patent Act protects newly developed plants in the same way that industrial inventions are protected. The patent owner is given legal protection for 17 years. During that time the owner is entitled to royalty for every offspring of the plant. Thus, development costs can be recouped and perhaps even a little profit made. Commercial rose nurseries often purchase licenses from inventors to propagate and sell particular cultivars.

The law requires that all patented roses be identified by a patent number engraved on a tag attached to the plant. Do not buy roses sold as patented unless they wear this identification tag. It is your guarantee that the plant will perform as the cultivar advertised.

CULTIVAR NAMES

When a rose is ready for its public debut, it needs a cultivar name. The hybridizer or distributing nursery chooses the name and, in the United States, registers it with the American Rose Society, designated as the U.S. National Rose Registration Center by the International Registration Authority for Roses.

The registration center reviews the name, along with complete descriptions of the plant in question, and rejects names that do not conform to provisions of the International Code. For example, names can be rejected if they are too similar to existing botanical or cultivar names. A name can be reused after 30 years if proof can be supplied that the original rose is extinct, not of historical importance, and was not used as a parent of an existing cultivar.

Top: In hybridizing greenhouse for miniatures, each yellow tag represents a cross; at right, the results of the work. Left: Impressive display of miniatures at Armstrong Nurseries' All-American Rose Garden in Ontario, CA.

ROSE SOCIETIES

Many gardeners who are captivated and develop a special interest in roses want to share their triumphs and problems with fellow rosarians. They also want to know of new cultivars being introduced and of new pest-control techniques and products, and to keep up to date on which roses in the marketplace are garnering the top awards. Rose societies offer these benefits and more to the interested gardener.

THE AMERICAN ROSE SOCIETY

For the dedicated rosarian in the United States, membership in the American Rose Society is a must. The society currently boasts more than 20,000 members, mostly amateurs, making it the largest special plant society in the United States. There are more than 350 local chapters and affiliated rose societies throughout the country. At its headquarters in Shreveport, Louisiana, the society has established The American Rose Center, a 118-acre park planted extensively in roses.

The American Rose Society provides the following benefits and services to its members:

☐ The monthly *American Rose* magazine is devoted to information on the culture, use, and history of roses.

☐ The *American Rose Annual* is a hardbound book sent to members, containing up-to-date, scientific information on roses and rose growing, beautiful color plates, and other articles of general interest to rose lovers.

☐ An extensive lending library of books on roses and related horticulture is maintained (the library can be used through the mail), and particular information on rose growing by individual members is provided.

☐ Cooperative research programs on rose-growing problems are maintained at various colleges and experimental stations.

☐ Two National Rose Conventions with meetings and rose shows are held each year. Assistance is given to district rose conferences and shows, as well as to local rose shows held by affiliated member societies throughout the country.

☐ Prizes and awards are granted for outstanding achievements in rose breeding.

☐ The International Horticultural Congress has delegated the American Rose Society as the International Registration Authority for Roses (IRAR). IRAR publishes monthly and annual lists of all new roses it registers.

☐ The society tabulates hundreds of individual reports from all over the country into an annual report of national ratings of all commercially available roses (see page 27). This *Handbook for Selecting Roses* is available to anyone at 35 cents per copy.

☐ An annual tabulation of the cultivars winning awards at rose shows is printed.

☐ The society maintains liaison with field societies and rosarians through strategically placed personnel called Consulting Rosarians. These individuals are available to help anyone with rose problems. A list is available from the society.

Right: Hybrid tea 'Olympiad', one of the 1984 All-America Rose Selections.

☐ Rose show supplies, books, program materials, and other data relative to complete operation of a rose society are available for purchase.

To start your membership in this active society, send $18 to American Rose Society, P.O. Box 30,000, Shreveport, LA 71130.

THE HERITAGE ROSES GROUP

The Heritage Roses Group was formed in 1975 as a fellowship of those who grow and enjoy old roses. Members receive *The Rose Letter* quarterly containing articles of interest on old roses, sources of plants, and cultural tips. A membership list is available for a small fee so you may contact other members in your area. Some areas have subgroups that meet two or three times a year.

Annual dues are $4 for members living in the United States, $4.25 for those living in Canada or Mexico. For membership write to the regional coordinator listed below who is nearest you, with a check payable to the coordinator.

Northeast
Lily Shohan
RD 1
Clinton Corners, NY 12514

Southwest
Miriam Wilkins
925 Galvin Drive
El Cerrito, CA 94530

Northcentral
Henry Najat, MD
Route 3
Monroe, WI 53566

Southcentral
Vickie Jackson
122 Bragg Street
New Orleans, LA 70124

Northwest
Jerry Fellman
947 Broughton Way
Woodburn, OR 97071

Southeast
Dr. Charles G. Jeremias
2103 Johnstone Street
Newberry, SC 29108

Roses in the Landscape

ROSES CAN PERFORM ALMOST ANY LANDSCAPING JOB IN THE GARDEN. HERE'S HOW TO CHOOSE HEALTHY, VIGOROUS PLANTS OF THE RIGHT TYPE AND VARIETY TO ASSURE YOU OF YEARS OF PLEASURE.

Roses are one of the most versatile plants available to the gardener. Don't shortchange them by thinking of them simply as bloom-producing machines; they can be an effective and integral part of your landscape. Because of the wide variety in their growth habits and sizes, roses can meet almost any landscaping challenge. And, unlike some other perennials, roses bloom the first year they're planted, so you won't have to wait long before enjoying their colorful displays. Use low-growing floribundas or miniatures to edge a walkway, or create a mass of summer color by filling a bed with hybrid teas. Many types of roses make excellent foundation plantings that can blend or contrast with the color of your house. Climbers can be trained on a screen to provide privacy, or against a house to cover an awkward architectural feature or to frame a window or door. Shrub and species roses, as well as the stately grandifloras, are excellent background plantings or can be used as tall hedges. Roses demand good drainage, so they can be especially effective on terraced hillsides. The smaller-size roses adapt well to container gardening, which means you will be able to move them about to create striking effects or to protect them from winter chill. Miniatures can even be grown inside to provide flowers all year round. It's unfortunate that roses aren't used more predominantly in landscaping; no other plant produces so many flowers so reliably over so long a period of time or has such an astounding variety of plant-growth habits and flower forms.

DESIGNING YOUR GARDEN

Many gardeners elect to keep all their rose plants in one section of the garden. The tradition of having a separate rose garden probably stems from the nineteenth-century practice of planting extensive gardens devoted to roses, just as other sections of the garden were devoted to particular types of plants such as herbs, water plants, and so forth. Concentrated displays of roses can produce a stunning and harmonious effect. You might consider it more convenient to have all your roses in one area when you are performing pruning, watering, and fertilizing chores. But as long as the site is right (which we shall discuss in a moment), there's no reason why you can't enjoy roses in all parts of your garden, as a focal point or as part of a colorful tapestry with other plants.

Miniatures are particularly versatile for blending with all parts of your garden and providing spots of color. You can use them as an edging around flower beds or the vegetable garden or mix them with such low-growing annuals as alyssum, calendula, and viola, and with other small, rock-garden plants.

Use roses throughout the landscape. Left: The brilliant 'Betty Prior' floribunda. Above: Showy hybrid tea 'Gavotte' (at left) with rich blooms of floribunda 'Cocorico'.

Above: Standard 'Garnette' is dramatically flanked by miniature tree rose 'Cricri' in this formal display.

Roses can be an integral part of your garden whether the design is formal or informal. A formal design is characterized by symmetry and straight or regularly curving lines. Elegant tree roses are an excellent choice for a formal garden: A row of them can seem like an honor guard of colorful heraldic soldiers at attention.

There is a type of garden planned for efficiency, without regard to design considerations. This is the cutting garden, where flowers are raised for shows or indoor arrangements. Usually located in an out-of-the-way part of the yard, the plants in a cutting garden should be arranged in such a way as to provide optimum spacing between them and to give you the utmost convenience in caring for them.

Sometimes a key word in landscaping is *restraint*. A *specimen* plant is one that is particularly lovely or spec-

tacular and is allowed to stand alone or dominate part of a landscape. A single strategically placed rosebush can be a bold accent that serves as a focal point or dominant element. When a rose stands alone, it should be special, with exceptional qualities of blooms, fragrance, or foliage. Whether it's a large shrub, a tree rose, a spectacular climber, or a hybrid tea of an unusual color, it should be positioned so that it can be viewed as an individual or where it will stand out among the other plants.

Below: White blossoms of Rosa gentiliana *lend an old-fashioned flavor to this informal bower.*
Right: Contrast highlights color, as here with
'Paul's Scarlet Climber'.

Top: Floribunda shrub rose 'Picasso'. Above: A tiered border—from top, 'Angel Face', 'Touch of Venus', 'Peace'.

REQUIREMENTS FOR PLANTING SITES

There are four considerations to keep in mind when choosing a spot in your garden to plant a rose: exposure to sun, exposure to wind, type of soil, and neighboring plants.

Sun. Roses should receive about 6 hours of full sun a day. In areas with intense summer heat, they will often appreciate some shade in the afternoon when the sun is hottest. A rose will grow in shade, but its growth will be spindly and unattractive, and it will produce few blossoms. The plant's susceptibility to rust and mildew diseases will also be increased in shade.

Wind. Don't plant roses in exposed locations where they are subject to prolonged hard winds. The wind damages blossoms and also causes rapid water evaporation from the foliage, making it necessary to water more often. A hedge of trees or shrubs can alleviate this problem.

Soil. Roses do best in slightly acid soil but generally will grow reasonably well in all but the most extreme types. The soil *must* be well drained at the same time that it retains moisture. In other words, the roots should not stand in water, but the soil around the roots should soak up some of the water for use by the roots. If you don't have well-drained soil in your garden, you can either bring in new soil and create a raised bed or amend your soil to create better drainage (see pages 30–31).

A hillside location always provides good drainage and helps to show off the roses, too. Make terraces, with a path on each terrace for tending and admiring the roses. Avoid low spots, where water collects after a rain.

Competition. Roses should not be planted too close to large trees and shrubs whose roots will compete with those of the rose for water and nutrients. Competition can be prevented by burying header boards 2–3 feet below the surface, thus keeping the roots of the tree or shrub from encroaching on the rose plant or plants. Some of the larger shrub roses do not need this protection, because they develop extensive enough root systems to compete with anything.

LAYOUT

Now that you've identified the appropriate places for planting roses in your garden, you'll have to start thinking about the type, size, and number of plants your garden *and* you can accommodate. If you want to plant one or two plants among other plants, you'll have to consider the eventual size of the roses and the mature size of neighboring plants (if they are not full grown). Allow enough space so that the plant will receive plenty of sun and there will be sufficient room for air to circulate around the plant even when it is fully grown. Remember that some of the old roses and shrub roses are very vigorous growers that need to be given corresponding latitude.

If you're planning on planting more than one or two roses, whether in a separate section of the garden or in just one bed, it's helpful to sketch to scale a plan of the planting area. Then you'll easily be able to plan enough space between each bush and move proposed plants around and let your imagination work. This initial extra effort will pay off because you won't have to move plants later or be required to spend time continually pruning so that your plants will have enough room.

Size. The chart below shows the approximate heights the different classes of roses reach when mature. These are not ironclad limits by any means: How much your roses grow depends on how warm or cold your climate is and how heavily the plants are pruned. Within the same class there are also variations in growth. Hybrid teas, for example, include low-, moderate-, and tall-growing cultivars.

Don't plant tall-growing cultivars in front of lower-growing types. If you do, you won't be able to enjoy the ones hidden in back! That may seem like an obvious admonition, but it's an easy mistake to make in the excitement of planning and planting.

As a rule of thumb, figure the spread of a rosebush to be about two-thirds its height. As we mentioned earlier, good air circulation around a plant lessens the possibility of disease. Another point to remember when you are planting is to allow plenty of room between two different cultivars. Different cultivars can present an unkempt appearance when entangled with each other. If you're planting more than one row of roses, stagger the placement of the plants in neighboring rows. This helps air circulation and provides a less rigid appearance.

If you won't be able to work on your roses from a path, leave a little extra room between plants so that you can move among the plants without being continually grabbed by thorns. You'll want to be able to step well clear of the base of the plant in order not to compact the earth and inhibit water drainage. Plant bushes at least 2 feet back from walkways so thorny branches won't snag passersby.

CLIMBER
6' to 20' tall; may have any type flowers; usually grown on fence, trellis, or post. Some are grafted.

GROWTH HABITS OF MODERN ROSES

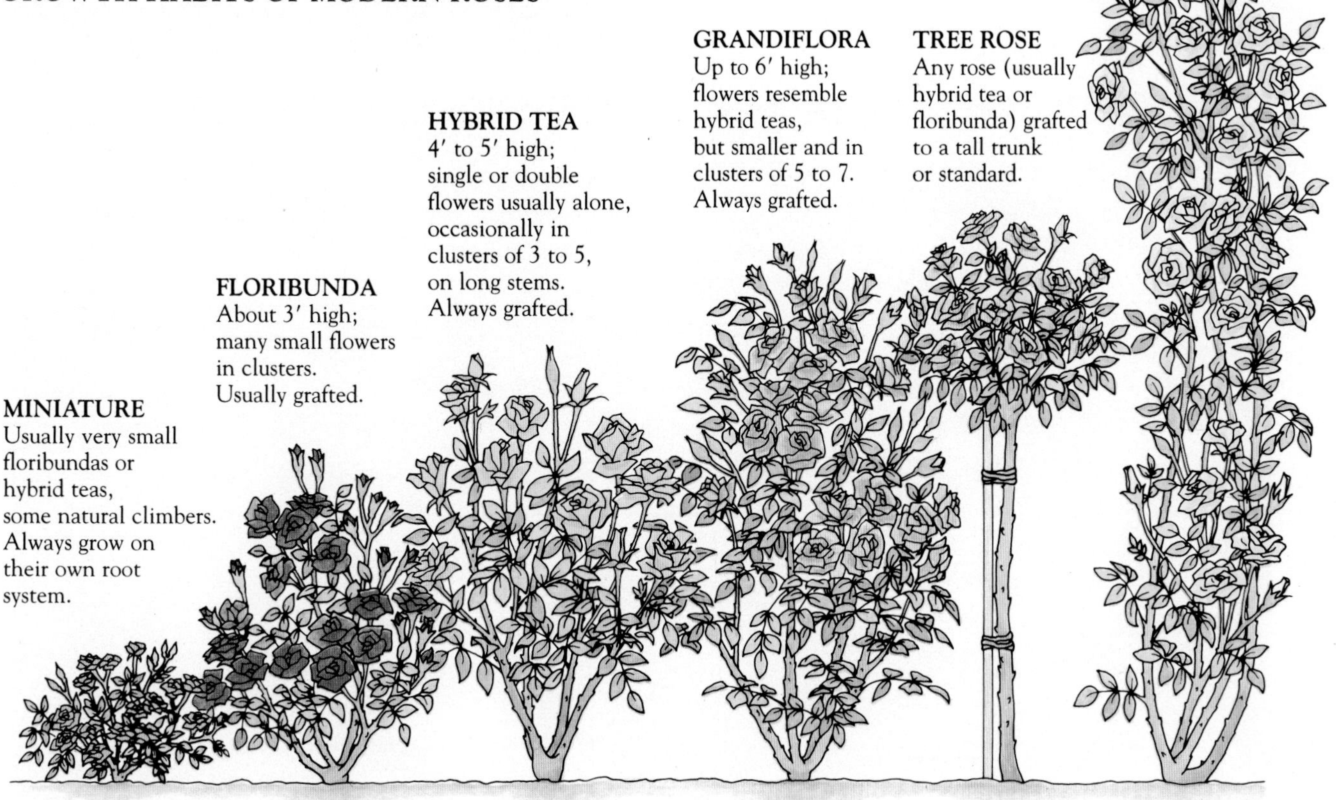

GRANDIFLORA
Up to 6' high; flowers resemble hybrid teas, but smaller and in clusters of 5 to 7. Always grafted.

TREE ROSE
Any rose (usually hybrid tea or floribunda) grafted to a tall trunk or standard.

HYBRID TEA
4' to 5' high; single or double flowers usually alone, occasionally in clusters of 3 to 5, on long stems. Always grafted.

FLORIBUNDA
About 3' high; many small flowers in clusters. Usually grafted.

MINIATURE
Usually very small floribundas or hybrid teas, some natural climbers. Always grow on their own root system.

Color. Many gardeners feel that all roses blend together, but some prefer a careful plan that eliminates clashing colors and creates a harmonious effect. Roses will give you a long seasonal parade of color, so plan a look you'll enjoy. Your preferences and imagination are the only limits here.

You may choose to create a monochromatic scheme by planting roses of a single color or several shades of one color. If so, choose a hue that blends well with the materials or color of the house, such as all shades of pink with a pink-toned brick house, or an all-white rose garden with a white frame house.

Carefully planned blends of two or three colors are preferred by some gardeners: Try yellows and oranges planted together, or pinks and reds. You can also design with two contrasting colors, such as lavender and orange or yellow and red.

Mixed colors lose their effectiveness in small areas, so it's usually best to plant three bushes of the same variety. If you have enough space, use bold splashes of color in every hue. If possible, plant at least two plants of the same color together so there will be small blocks of different colors rather than little spots. In this manner you can create a riot of color, which you can temper with a white rose, very effective in providing a quiet accent.

Bright, warm colors planted at the rear of a garden make the space appear smaller; cool colors make the garden seem longer or deeper.

Most blooms are best highlighted against a background of dark greenery or a fence or wall painted a dark color. Some plants with deep-pink blossoms, however, need a light-colored backdrop for their rich colors to be displayed to the best advantage.

For help in your planning, refer to the lists of cultivars arranged by color on page 89.

Spotlight roses against a fence or foliage. Below: China rose 'Hermosa'. Bottom: Floribunda 'Angel Face'.

ROSES IN CONTAINERS

Planting roses in containers rather than in the ground allows the gardener even more flexibility for integrating roses into the landscape. Container-grown roses can be placed almost anywhere you wish and, of course, are easily repositioned if you so desire.

Frame your entryway with proud standards for a special party. Enjoy spots of color and fragrance courtesy of roses on your patio or deck. Create displays of color in window boxes with individually potted miniature roses. Bring color to eye level with hanging baskets of small roses.

Containers are also a boon to many gardeners who live in apartments and townhouses and don't have ground to work in. Don't forget that miniatures can be grown exclusively indoors, in a bright, sunny window or under artificial lights.

Roses in containers also have the advantage that they can be moved into a sheltered and heated location to protect them from winter chill. Large pots and planters can be moved by means of a dolly or a small platform with casters. Gardeners in warmer climates might want to move their roses in containers to an inconspicuous part of the garden when the plants are dormant and bare of foliage.

Small hybrid teas, standards, floribundas, polyanthas, and miniatures are the best roses to use for small containers. But with large-size (5-gallon or larger) containers you can accommodate the large hybrid teas, grandifloras, and most of the old roses. Using the tall-growing roses in large containers in a semipermanent location, such as a rooftop garden, where mobility is not so important and winter protection is sufficient, will result in less back-breaking lifting, pushing, and pulling. An advantage of floribundas and polyanthas is that their blooms are produced in clusters, giving the effect of larger sweeps of color per plant.

Use roses to define space or create visual depth. Top: 'Nevada' shrub rose. Above: Crimson floribunda 'Europeana'. Right: 'Dwarf King' mini brightens a patio.

CHOOSING A CULTIVAR

Now that you've decided where to plant your roses, how big you want them to get, and what color blossoms they'll have, you can get down to deciding which cultivars to plant. There is an astounding array of cultivars available in almost every conceivable combination of attributes and characteristics. We've listed over 250 different cultivars in the "Encyclopedia of Roses" on pages 61–88. Don't be overwhelmed by the large number; once you've decided on the characteristics you want in a plant, the list becomes more manageable.

When choosing a cultivar, there are a number of questions you should ask yourself: How much time will I have to care for the plants? How much winter protection will plants need in my climate? Is fragrance an important criterion? Do I want color mainly in the garden or flowers to cut for indoor arrangements? Will different shades of color go as well together as I think? Let's take a look at these considerations.

MAINTENANCE

All roses need *some* care, but some need substantially less than others. On page 91 there's a list of roses that are not fussy and can thrive with a minimum of care. If you wish to explore beyond this listing, pick cultivars that are disease-resistant. That way you won't have to worry about being eternally vigilant regarding the control and prevention of diseases. Make sure you give plants described as "vigorous" lots of room to grow; otherwise you'll have to have your pruning clippers always at the ready.

Revitalize home landscaping ideas with a visit to a public garden, such as this one at Hershey, PA.

CLIMATE

Consider what the usual coldest winter temperatures are in your area. In severe winter climates it's necessary to provide some protection for your roses (see pages 44–45), but even if you protect them, don't choose plants described as "very tender." Some roses perform well where summers are hot and dry, others where summers are hot and humid, or cool. We've given our recommendations for these climates in the "Encyclopedia of Roses".

DISEASE RESISTANCE

Roses that are particularly resistant to all or some diseases are usually so described. It's likely that with these plants you won't have to cope with diseases, but it's not impossible that they will be attacked. Similarly, your plants will not necessarily be subject to disease if the plant is not described as being disease-resistant, though you probably should take precautions (see page 40). Certain diseases are often concentrated in certain areas. Talk to friends and neighbors who grow roses about their experiences to determine if a particular disease is troublesome in your area. Or seek the counsel of your local rose society members. On page 92 we give lists of of hybrid teas, floribundas, and grandifloras that are particularly resistant to blackspot and mildew.

FRAGRANCE

One of the first reactions of most people who pause to admire a rose is to lean over and take a sniff. If there is a fragrance, the enjoyment seems to be complete. If this is also a large part of your pleasure in roses, you can choose from among many fragrant roses. 'Chrysler Imperial' and 'Peace', two very popular hybrid teas, are very fragrant; among the old roses, the damasks are particularly noted for their rose fragrance. A selection of fragrant roses is given on page 91.

CUT FLOWERS

You'll probably want to cut some of your flowers and bring them inside to enjoy. (See pages 55–56 for procedures to assure their longevity.) All roses can be picked for indoor arrangements, but hybrid teas and grandifloras are favored for formal arrangements because of their long, straight stems. A list of cultivars that produce long-lasting blossoms for indoor arrangements is given on page 92.

SHADES OF COLORS

Remember that within any one color classification, such as red or gold, there is a wide range of intensity and quality of color. If you are juxtaposing or blending different colors, make sure that the shades you choose will give the effect you want.

PUBLIC ROSE GARDENS

You can learn a great deal from visits to public rose gardens. There you can be inspired by landscaping ideas, see new introductions and tests, smell and touch unusual or hard-to-find varieties, and study old-fashioned cultivars. All show off their best qualities in response to the particular climate of the garden.

Look for roses you like. Observe their growing habits to see how the plants can fit your own landscape needs. Let specimen blooms guide you in selecting the color, fragrance, and size you want for your own garden. Jot down the names so later you can order or find the species or cultivar that does just what you want. A resident horticulturist is usually happy to answer any questions.

In addition, many commercial rose growers and retailers have display gardens that are open to the public. Check the descriptions with the listings given on page 92. It's always best to call ahead before you visit.

ROSE SHOWS

Local chapters of the American Rose Society present frequent local and regional shows in which members compete for awards. You won't get to inspect the plants, but you'll be able to observe and smell many near-perfect flowers. You will also have a chance to get information and opinions from the rose gardeners in attendance. Write to the national society office (see page 17) for information on the nearest local chapter.

AWARDS AND RATINGS

Awards and ratings are other guides for selecting cultivars. Award-winning and top-rated roses are sure to be exceptional in a number of performance categories.

All-America Rose Selections. After the passage of the Plant Patent Act in 1930, large numbers of roses, some of very poor quality, were patented and sold to the public. To supply the rose-buying public with objective data on the best roses of new introductions, major rose growers formed

Each All-America Rose Selection—such as the hybrid tea 'Electron'—must undergo extensive testing.

in 1938 a nonprofit group, All-America Rose Selections (AARS), to recognize outstanding new introductions.

Each new introduction is subjected to rigorous, standardized observation over a two-year period in 23 test gardens in the varied climates of the United States. Judges rate each rose under submission according to 14 different categories: novelty, bud form, flower form, color on opening, color at end of bloom, substance (texture of the petals), fragrance, flower stem or cluster formation, growth habit, vigor of growth, foliage, disease resistance, flowering effect, and overall value. The rose or roses with the highest ratings are then declared the winners. Most of the AARS winners for the last 15 years, plus some older favorites, are included in the "Encyclopedia of Roses" starting on page 61.

The AARS also distributes to affiliated public rose gardens new introductions the year before they are listed in catalogs, which allows you to inspect new roses in bloom the year that they are introduced.

American Rose Society ratings. Every three years the ARS surveys its membership for ratings on roses grown by members in all parts of the country. Varieties and cultivars are rated on a scale of 1 to 10, and the results are published annually in the *Handbook for Selecting Roses*, available from the society for 35 cents. Ratings for individual roses are given in the "Encyclopedia of Roses," beginning on page 61. The ARS breaks down the ratings qualitatively in the following ranges:

10.0	Perfect (not yet achieved)
9.9–9.0	Outstanding
8.9–8.0	Excellent
7.9–7.0	Good
6.9–6.0	Fair
5.9 and lower	Of questionable value

Keep in mind, however, that a low rating does not necessarily mean that a rose is a dud. It may still have many fine attributes that make it worth growing, such as fragrance or hardiness, though other characteristics are less than perfect. Rating scores may also be lowered because the rose does less well in some parts of the country than it does in others.

Other awards. The ARS sponsors an Award for Excellence for miniature roses.

In 1961 Dr. James Alexander Gamble established a fund with the ARS to encourage the development of fragrant roses. The James Alexander Gamble Rose Fragrance Medal is awarded to roses with a nationwide rating of 8.0 or better that are "strongly and delightfully fragrant." Winners of the award, only seven so far, are indicated in the list of fragrant roses on page 91.

The Gold Medal Certificate was established by the American Rose Society in 1948 to recognize those roses that have shown the best performance over a period of 5 years. To date, only 13 have been chosen: from the hybrid teas, 'Chrysler Imperial', 'Peace', and 'Tropicana'; among the grandifloras, 'Carrousel', 'Montezuma', and 'Queen Elizabeth'; from the floribundas, 'Fashion', 'Frensham', 'Spartan', and 'Vogue'; and representing the large-flowered climbers, shrubs, and miniatures, 'City of York', 'Golden Wings', and 'Toy Clown', respectively.

Planting and Care

IF YOU FOLLOW THE SIMPLE
TECHNIQUES OF PLANTING AND
REGULAR CARE OUTLINED
HERE, YOUR EFFORTS WILL BE
AMPLY REWARDED BY PRODUCTIVE,
HEALTHY PLANTS AND BLOOMS.

This chapter is a summary of techniques used to care for roses. It is not gospel. If you gather 10 avid rosarians together, it's more than likely that you will get 10 different answers to the same question on a particular cultural practice. All the answers will be valid—for each gardener and his or her garden. You will find the methods that work best for you and your garden through experience —including, quite likely, a few failures.

Roses *can* survive neglect and even abuse, but the results will not be pleasing—a few small blossoms supported by ratty looking, tangled foliage. A rosebush with a full quota of clean leaves and with a constant supply of moisture and nutrients will produce more than twice as many blooms as one scantily fed and only partially protected from pests, diseases, and the elements.

CHOOSING HEALTHY PLANTS
To get off to a good start with your rose plants, it pays to spend a little time and effort—and sometimes a little more money—to choose healthy, vigorous plants that will perform to their full potential.

Left: Expertly pruned bloom-covered 'DeMeaux' dwarf shrub rose. Above: 'Parade', a vigorous low-climbing rose with hybrid tea type flowers, here is shaped to embellish a fence.

Rose plants are available either bare-root during the winter or growing in containers. Either type of plant, if carefully chosen, will produce good roses over a long lifetime. Your best bet is to purchase plants from reputable mail-order suppliers or local nurseries. You're better off buying from people who sell roses year after year and stand behind the quality of their plants. Inspect plants carefully before you buy, and be cautious of bargains, especially those offered by retail stores where nursery plants are a sideline. It's likely that the plants have had less-than-perfect care, and they may be permanently affected. You will have a considerable investment of time and energy in each rose plant, so it's advisable to spend a little extra money to assure high quality in the plants you buy.

BUYING CONTAINER-GROWN PLANTS
Container-grown plants have a couple of advantages over bare-root plants. You can see what the plant will look like when it is growing (and sometimes blooming). Container-grown plants are also somewhat easier to plant. However, they are generally more expensive than bare-root plants, and fewer varieties are available. When buying a container-grown plant, examine the foliage and canes carefully. The plant should be healthy and vigorous looking. There should be no die back or twiggy growth, evidence that the plant has been growing in the container for over a year.

Container-grown roses are often available all year in nurseries, but it's best not to buy them after midsummer, when it is possible that they have become pot-bound. Steer clear of roses planted in small (less than 5-gallon) pots for the same reason.

Miniature roses are almost always sold in containers. They can be safely bought throughout the year, since they are often grown in greenhouses, starting at different times of the year. Select plants with healthy green foliage that is not all in a tangle.

BUYING BARE-ROOT PLANTS
Bare-root roses are shipped and sold while the plants are dormant and need only be kept cool and moist. All mail-order suppliers ship bare-root plants, and they will arrange for delivery at the best planting time for your area or whenever you specify.

Bare-root rose plants are graded as 1, 1½, and 2, according to the size and number of canes. If you're willing to pay the price for the best possible blooms, buy number 1 grade plants with three or four heavy canes at least ⅜ inch in diameter, hybrid teas and grandifloras 18 inches in height, and floribundas 15 inches. To meet the number 1 grade, these classes of roses must have at least two canes of the specified length, and branching must begin no more than 3 inches above the bud union. Number 1 polyanthas are required to have at least four canes 12 inches or longer. Climbers must have at least three canes 24 inches or longer to qualify for the top grade.

In nurseries, bare-root plants are usually kept in boxes of moist sawdust, so you can inspect the roots as well as the canes. Examine canes to be sure that the wood is not dry and shriveled. The plant should be well shaped, with no deformed growth, abnormal swellings, and discolorations on canes or roots, which may be symptoms of disease. Bark on the canes should be firm, plump, and green. The root system should be sturdy and fibrous, with several firm, well-branched roots.

Canes are often wrapped in plastic to retain their moisture, and the plastic acts as a greenhouse, encouraging

Check roots and canes of bare-root roses before buying.

the plants to start growing. As soon as you get your plants home, remove the plastic from around the canes and store the plants as described below. If the canes do start to sprout before you've gotten the plant into the ground, pinch back the shoots to ¼ inch, to prevent the evaporation of moisture from the plants.

CARE UNTIL PLANTING
Your rose plants should be kept cool and moist until you are able to plant them. They must be kept moist or they will die, and if they aren't kept cool, they will begin to grow and there will be more risk of injury to foliage and roots when you do plant them.

If the ground is not frozen and can be worked, heel your bare-root plants into a trench. Dig a trench in a shady spot with one sloping side, and lay the plants on this side with the roots at the bottom. Cover both the roots and the canes with earth and moisten the soil thoroughly.

You can also keep your plants by packing the roots in a moisture-retaining material, such as sawdust, peat moss, or perlite, and storing them in a cool (but not freezing) place. Make sure the material remains damp; if it dries out, soak it in water and then squeeze out excess moisture. Wet newspapers or burlap laid over the canes will further reduce evaporation from the plant.

PREPARING THE SITE
Roses perform best when they receive full sunshine all day or at least 6 hours of direct sunlight daily from spring through the fall. Morning sun is essential; partial afternoon shade is acceptable.

There should be air movement through the foliage to keep it dry and discourage diseases. Plant away from large trees or shrubs that compete for nutrients, moisture, and sunlight.

DRAINAGE
Roses need good drainage. If the desired site doesn't drain well, you can modify it in several ways.

If you are preparing a large rose bed, you can dig a large trench beneath the planting site and bury a drain tile or pipe in coarse gravel. Drain openings should be covered with asphalt roofing paper to prevent soil from washing in and clogging the holes. The pipe should be slightly slanted toward a ditch, storm sewer, or dry well.

Raised beds. An easier solution might be to build a raised bed. In very moist areas build up a bed at least 16–20 inches high. Beds for miniature roses can be half as high. The side construction can be redwood or masonry framing, old railway ties, even stone or brick. Fill the enclosure with soil mix made from the recipe given below. In addition to giving your roses excellent drainage, you'll find raised beds to be a convenient height for gardening chores. A seat cap lets you sit down beside the roses to work.

If you live in an area with severe winters, be sure to plant your roses at least 12 inches from the sides of a raised bed. This allows enough soil to act as insulation for the roots.

Planting sites on slopes usually have excellent drainage, but consider the possibility of erosion before you plant. Terracing can prevent erosion problems. Terracing is merely a modified raised-bed approach.

MODIFYING SOIL DRAINAGE

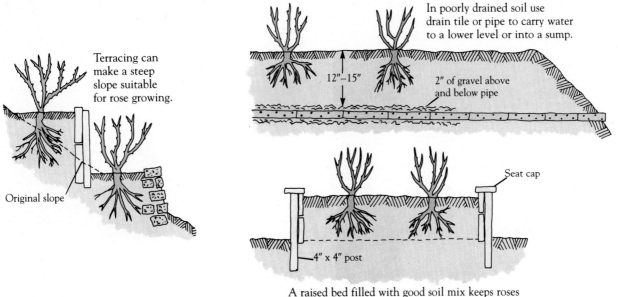

Terracing can make a steep slope suitable for rose growing.

Original slope

In poorly drained soil use drain tile or pipe to carry water to a lower level or into a sump.

12"–15"

2" of gravel above and below pipe

Seat cap

4" x 4" post

A raised bed filled with good soil mix keeps roses out of heavy, rocky, or poorly drained native soil.

SOIL

Roses do well in a wide range of soils but prefer loamy soil with a high humus content to a depth of at least 2 feet. A recipe for an ideal growing medium that you can use to fill raised beds is:

5 parts (by volume) loamy soil

4 parts organic matter, such as compost or leaf mold, dehydrated cow manure, peat moss, or shredded bark (all available from garden centers)

1 part builder's sand

Add 3–4 pounds of superphosphate per 100 square feet of soil surface for stronger root development.

If you're planting bushes individually and your soil is good, dig holes 16–20 inches wide and 14–18 inches deep. Work some organic matter and sand into the soil you have excavated. Use the same principle for a large bed of roses. For best results, most experts advise preparing the soil area 3–6 months before planting the roses.

If you have extremely poor soil, remove all existing soil to a depth of 16–20 inches and replace it altogether with a mixture of good loam, sand, and organic matter in the proportions given above.

Roses grow best in a slightly acid soil with a pH of 6.0–6.5. If you suspect your soil is alkaline, make a soil test. If your soil is too alkaline, you can make it more acidic by working agricultural sulphur into the soil. How much you should add depends on the texture of your soil. To lower the pH of 100 square feet of soil by 1 point (from 7.5 to 6.5, for example): if you have light, sandy loam, apply 1 pound of sulphur; if you have medium-weight loam, apply 1½ pounds; if you have clay loam, apply 2 pounds of sulphur.

If you are preparing a large bed and there have been problems with nematodes or soil-borne disease in your area, preplanting fumigation of the soil might be a good idea. The most satisfactory fumigant for roses is methyl bromide, a gas released under an airtight cover. Check with local professional pest-control experts about applying the fumigant.

PLANTING ROSES IN THE GARDEN

Roses bought in containers can be planted in the garden at any time during the spring, summer, or fall. If you plant during hot weather, however, be sure to give the newly planted rose plenty of water. Be sure to check vigilantly that it has enough moisture for at least 6 weeks after planting. (For instructions on watering newly planted roses, see page 37.)

Planting times for bare-root roses, however, vary according to the severity of the winter climate in your part of the country. If temperatures in your area do not fall below 10°F, you can plant whenever you buy your dormant plants. If the minimum winter temperatures are between 10°F and −10° F, plant only in the early spring or late fall. If the coldest temperatures in your region fall below −10°F, plant only in the early spring.

In cold-winter regions you can theoretically plant whenever the ground has thawed out enough to be worked easily. Generally, the best advice is to get a plant into the ground as early as possible to give the root system a head start before the foliage forms. But if you often get severe spring freezes, wait until the danger is past. A newly planted young rose can be killed by a severe drop in temperature.

Don't be tempted to plant bare-root roses on windy winter days when the temperature may drop below freezing. The combination of the cold with the drying wind can *be* fatal to the tender new plants and *feel* almost fatal to the gardener.

PLANTING BARE-ROOT ROSES

Before planting, soak your bare-root roses in water for a few hours (but no longer than 24 hours). Keep them in water until you are just ready to plant. Trim any roots that have been broken.

After preparing the hole as outlined earlier, position the plant in the hole. The roots should not be twisted or curved. If one or two roots are too long for the hole you have dug, you can prune them to 8–10 inches long so they will fit.

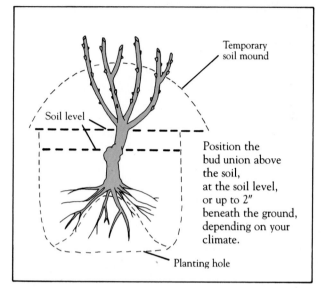

Position the plant vertically by laying your spade handle or a stake across the hole to align the bud union (the knoblike protuberance on the stem just below the canes) with the level of the soil. The bud union is the point at which the cultivar was grafted to the rootstock, and it is particularly sensitive to extreme cold. The proper position of the bud union in planting is a point of disagreement among rosarians, even those within the same region. The rule of thumb is that the bud union should be 2 inches below the soil level in severe winter areas (lows below −10°F). Place it slightly above the soil level in cold winter areas (lows between 10°F and −10°F). In mild winter climates position the bud union 2 inches above the ground.

Build a cone of soil mixture in the center of the hole to support the spread-out roots and to hold the plant so that the bud union is maintained at the optimum level. With the plant in position, add about two-thirds of the soil mix around the sides and then fill the hole with water. Let it soak in completely. Fill in the rest of the hole around the roots with soil mix, firm the soil gently by hand, and settle the soil with a second soaking of water.

Mound the soil at least 8 inches high around the plant. You may have to get extra soil for this. Moisten again. This mound gives protection from drying winds and warm sun and provides additional moisture for the developing plant.

Leave the mound until new growth is 1 or 2 inches long and all danger of frost is past. You can gradually acclimate the plant by washing away an inch or 2 of the mound each day.

Tree roses should be securely staked after planting. Place the stake on the south side of the plant to provide partial shade for the trunk, which is sensitive to hot sun.

1. *Healthy bare-root rose ready for planting displays well-branched root system.*

2. *Hole should accommodate root system without crowding.*

3. *Build soil cone to support roots; handle aids placement.*

4. *Fill hole with enriched, slightly acid soil, hand-pressing to remove air pockets and to stabilize plant.*

7. *When an inch or 2 of new growth is established and frost danger has passed, begin to remove soil around canes.*

5. *Saturate soil thoroughly by filling hole with water.*

6. *Soil mound protects plant and helps it retain moisture.*

8. *Wash away a bit of the mound at each watering.*

PLANTING CONTAINER-GROWN ROSES

Dig a hole 5–6 inches wider and deeper than the container in which the rose is growing. Mix soil thoroughly and place about 6 inches of amended soil in the bottom of the hole.

Remove the plant from the container. If it is a metal can, the nursery will slit the sides for you to make removal easier. Place the rose in the hole at the same level it was growing in the container. Add the soil mixture around the root soil.

If the rose is not well rooted in the container, to avoid disturbing the rootball, cut out and remove the bottom of the container and carefully set the plant in the hole at the proper height. Cut the sides of the container and loosely fill the rest of the hole with soil mix. Remove the sides of the container and the soil will remain intact around the roots. Water thoroughly to settle the soil, fill the hole with soil once more, and water again.

While the backfill soil is still wet and soupy, make final adjustments to the plant's position. Lift it if it is too deep, or tip it upright if it is leaning. Since the rose is already growing, there is no need to mound soil as in bare-root planting. Keep the plant well watered until it is established.

TRANSPLANTING ROSES

Transplant roses in the early spring or late fall when they are dormant, but while the ground is workable.

Prepare the new planting site as you would for planting a rose bought in a container. Soak the soil around the plant overnight so you can dig the plant with as much earth as possible to minimize root disturbance. Prune large bushes back by one-half to make them easier to handle.

The next day dig up the plant, disturbing the roots as little as possible, and position it in the new hole and firm soil around the roots. Water the plant well.

PLANTING ROSES GROWN IN CONTAINERS

1. Dig a hole and place amended soil in bottom.

3. Fill hole loosely with soil, water thoroughly, fill hole again, and water again.

2. Remove plant from container and place in hole.

4. Keep well watered until plant is established.

PLANTING ROSES IN CONTAINERS

Select a container that gives the root system as much room as possible. For most floribundas and small hybrid teas, a container must be at least 14–16 inches in diameter (or on a square diagonal) and 18–20 inches deep. Five-gallon nursery containers are about the minimum size for most roses other than miniatures. You'll find, however, that most roses will grow much more lushly in larger containers. A plant will become rootbound and constricted in a small container, resulting in loss of leaves, poor flower production, or even death.

Wooden tubs and boxes are excellent for roses. Moisture can evaporate through the sides, and the soil stays cool. The common, porous terra-cotta pots are simple, handsome, and readily available, but plants tend to dry out more quickly in these than in glazed pottery. Plastic pots and metal containers, especially dark-colored ones, can heat up in direct sun, causing the roots on the sunny side of the container to die.

Whatever your choice in containers, be sure to provide good drainage or the roots of the plant may rot. Several holes made in the bottom of the container are a good idea. Cleats, casters, feet, wooden x's, or small pieces of brick positioned underneath the containers will keep them from standing in water.

Use a growing medium composed of 3 parts sandy loam and 1 part organic matter such as peat moss or leaf mold. Good results are also obtained with any of the soil-less mixes, available ready-mixed in large bags.

You can use containers to plant either bare-root bushes or plants already growing in cardboard containers or nursery cans. Roses that already have a head start growing in containers seem to adapt best to container gardening. Perhaps it's because their roots have already adjusted to a confined space. Bare-root plants, in contrast, come directly from fields.

If you choose a porous clay pot, soak it for about 30 minutes before you plant in it, so the clay won't rob the roots of soil moisture. When you're ready to plant, place curved pieces of broken crockery over the drainage holes to keep soil from washing through. If the pot will be set on the ground, use pieces of screen instead of pottery to keep worms from crawling into the pot.

Add a few scoops of soil, and set the plant at the correct growing height, just as you would if the plant were to be grown in the ground. For easier watering leave 1½–2 inches between the soil level and the top of the pot. Continue adding soil, packing it down well to eliminate air pockets. After you have filled the pot to the soil level, soak the soil thoroughly.

You can cover the topsoil with a mulch, plant a shallow-rooted ground cover such as Scotch moss or baby's-tears, or add a few seedling annuals to dress up the container and provide color before the roses start to bloom.

Place the container where the plant will get at least 6 hours of direct morning or midday sunlight. If the bush leans toward the sun, find a place with more hours of sun per day and rotate the pot every few days to ensure that the plant grows evenly. Keep the plant away from light-colored walls during hot sunny days. Reflected heat can cause foliage burn.

GROWING ROSES IN CONTAINERS

1. Place broken crockery over drainage holes.

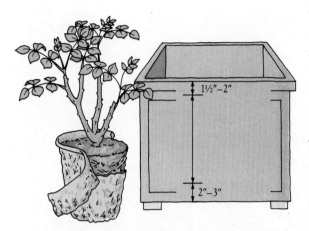

2. Add soil, set in the plant at the correct height. Pour in more soil, leaving 1½" to 2" watering space at the top of the pot.

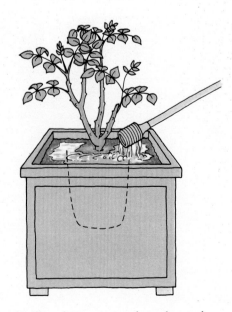

3. Pack soil well to eliminate air pockets, then soak thoroughly.

1. *Miniature rose will grow more vigorously in ground.*
2. *Set plant slightly deeper in hole than it was in pot.*

3. *Tamp down soil around roots to eliminate air pockets.*
4. *After planting, water thoroughly by filling basin.*

5. *Permanent labels identify each of these miniatures.*

MINIATURE ROSES

Whether planted in the garden or in containers, miniature roses enjoy the same soil and care as their larger relatives. Since miniatures grow on their own roots (that is, they're not grafted), you don't have to worry about the position of a bud union when you plant. Whether you plant in a pot or in the ground, set the rosebush slightly deeper than it originally grew.

When planting in the garden, dig holes 8–10 inches deep; most cultivars should be spaced about 10–12 inches apart. Make sure the roses are separated from large plants that can rob them of much-needed sunshine and moisture.

When you read catalog descriptions of miniature plant sizes, remember that these are usually based on indoor or greenhouse pot culture, where size is regulated by restricted root growth. Although the flowers remain tiny, many of the miniature plants will grow to 2½–3 feet when planted in the ground, especially in warm climates. To keep the bushes small, you'll need to prune them back severely every year.

Miniature roses can be planted in pots 4–10 inches in diameter. If you will be growing them indoors, use a packaged synthetic soil mix instead of garden soil to prevent the spread of pests or diseases.

LABEL YOUR PLANTS

Patented roses are sold with name tags attached, but the wire attachment can cut into the cane as it grows. Remove it at planting time and attach the label to a stake near the plant. You can, of course, fashion your own label in the style of your choice.

In addition to name tags near the plant in your garden, make a diagram of your landscape and write in the names of the roses, dates planted, sources, and any other information you wish to include. This may be valuable in the years to come, especially to identify a rose whose label has been lost or if you want to have a record of the age of your plants.

MULCHING

The soil around roses needs just enough cultivation to eliminate weeds and prevent a hard surface crust from forming. Cultivating soil to a shallow level, only 1–1½ inches deep, will prevent injury to roots that may be growing close to the surface. Deep cultivation can destroy these feeder roots.

Weeds can be controlled by pulling them by hand from damp soil, making sure that you get the root along with the top.

But there's a simple way to cut back on both these chores and obtain other advantages as well. Apply a mulch around your rose plants or over a whole bed.

Mulches can be either organic, such as bark, or inorganic, such as black plastic. A mulch acts as an extra layer between the soil and air, slowing the evaporation of moisture from the soil and preventing the formation of a hard crust at soil level. Additionally, the layer of mulch keeps sunlight from reaching the soil and stimulating weed growth.

The accompanying chart lists the advantages and disadvantages of various materials you can use as a mulch. Not the least advantage of most mulches is the neat, attractive appearance they add to your rose beds. Note that organic

MULCHING MATERIALS

Material	Comments
Bark	Available commercially in chip form or finely ground. Very attractive and long lasting.
Grass clippings or hay	Probably the most available mulch, but unattractive. Let dry before spreading. Repeated use builds up reserve of available nutrients which lasts for years.
Gravel or stone chips	Not too attractive with roses. Extremely durable, holds down weeds, but does not supply plant nutrients or humus.
Mushroom compost (spent)	This material is often available in areas where commercial mushrooms are produced. It is usually inexpensive, with a good color that blends into the landscape.
Newspaper	Readily available. Can be used shredded or in sheets, held in place by rocks, bricks, or soil. Cover with more attractive material. Builds humus, and ink contains beneficial trace elements.
Peat moss	Attractive at first, tends to lose esthetic appeal with age. Available, but expensive for large areas. Compacts and sheds rain water. Should be kept moist at all times.
Pine needles	Will not mat down. Fairly durable. Potential fire hazard.
Black plastic film	Excellent mulch, but unattractive. Can be covered with thin layer of bark. Punch holes for penetration of water. Eliminates weeds entirely.
Rotted manure	May contain weed seeds.
Sawdust, wood chips, or shavings	Low in plant nutrients, decompose slowly, tend to pack down. Rose foliage may yellow; additional nitrogen will correct the problem. Well-rotted material preferred. Can be fresh if nitrate of ammonia or nitrate of soda is supplemented at the rate of one pound per 100 square feet. Keep away from building foundations; may attract termites.
Straw	Long-lasting. Depletes nitrogen, but furnishes considerable potassium.
Tree leaves (whole or shredded)	Excellent source of humus. Rot rapidly, high in nutrients.

Organic redwood bark mulch defines this 'Pink Grootendorst' shrub rose as a landscape specimen, reduces weeding chores, and retains soil moisture.

mulches add nutrients to the soil as they decompose and create a looser soil texture.

After planting, apply 2–4 inches of mulch around the plants, leaving a circle of bare soil 10–12 inches in diameter around the base of each plant so water can reach it easily. Leave the mulch in place all year long; it acts as an insulator during the winter as well as the summer, preventing rapid temperature changes in the soil.

If you have experienced problems with a fungus disease, however, remove all the old mulch and replace it with clean, fresh material in early fall.

WATERING

One thing rose gardeners all agree on is that you can't give a rose too much water. Though moisture should be retained by the soil, drainage must be excellent so that the roots are not standing in water. See page 31 for methods to correct poor soil drainage. Rose foliage will wilt if there is insufficient moisture. During the growing season, rose leaves should always be turgid.

It's difficult to prescribe how much or how often to water. The frequency of watering as well as the amount depend on soil type, climate, and the growth stage of the rose. More water is needed when the soil is loose and sandy, when it's heavily compacted, when the air is hot and dry, or when new plants are becoming established.

You should be particularly attentive to newly planted roses if your spring is particularly warm or early. Their root systems may not have developed enough to provide sufficient moisture to the growing foliage stimulated by the warmth of the sun.

Normally a rose should receive the equivalent of 1 to 2 inches of rainfall per week, all at one time, starting in early spring and continuing through the fall. Hot and dry weather may call for watering every 3 or 4 days. Porous soils benefit from additional deep soakings.

In the early spring, water roses from overhead with a sprinkler or sprayer to prevent the canes from drying. When foliage growth begins, apply the water directly to the soil. An occasional overhead sprinkling thereafter will keep the foliage clean, but sprinkle only in the early morning so the leaves have a chance to dry out by evening.

When you water, water deeply, soaking the soil to a depth of 16–18 inches. A light sprinkling is worse than no water at all. Frequent light applications result in shallow root systems that will not physically support the plant and will require continued frequent waterings. Lightly watered plants are, in addition, subject to injury from cultivation or fertilizer burns.

If you're not sure how deeply you're watering, water for a measured period of time and then dig down near the plant and measure the depth to which the soil is damp. If the soil is damp only to a depth of 8 inches, for example, you'll probably have to water about twice as long as you did.

To irrigate deeply, some people build a dike around the entire bed; others prefer forming a basin around each rosebush. Then flood the bed or basin with water and let it slowly soak into the soil. Use a bubbler attachment on the end of the hose to prevent a strong stream of water from eroding the soil or splashing the foliage with dirt or mulch. The most efficient system is slow-drip irrigation at the base of each plant. Flooding the whole bed is wasteful because most of the water runs off or evaporates and what remains penetrates the soil only a few inches. A soaker hose, or one of the methods illustrated below, can provide deep soaking to moisten the soil to the required depth. It saves you time, energy, and even money, because less water is used in the long run.

WATERING ROSES IN CONTAINERS

The task of watering is critical for container plants because they have much less soil from which to draw moisture. A rose that lacks moisture will be stunted, and if it is denied often or for a long period, it will die. Check the amount of moisture deep in the pot at least every couple of days during the summer and every day when the weather is very hot or windy.

Wood, plastic, and glazed-pottery containers lose less moisture to the surrounding air than unglazed pots. Placing one container inside another will insulate and cut down on moisture loss. Be sure the outside container has drainage holes so that roots are not standing in water.

WATERING YOUR ROSES

Water basins efficiently with spaghetti tubes that extend from a pipe near the center of the bed. Pipes may be hidden with mulch.

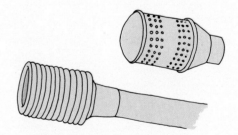

Bubbler hose attachments prevent a strong stream of water from splashing soil on the foliage.

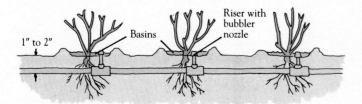

PVC pipe may be set a couple of inches beneath the soil surface and near to each rosebush where special risers dispense water right at the roots.

FERTILIZING

Most roses need regular applications of fertilizer to achieve their optimum growth and flower production. A healthy, well-fed plant will also strongly resist attacks of pests and diseases and be able to weather severe winter cold.

The rate and frequency of fertilizer application and the appropriate fertilizer to use depend on the type of soil in your garden. Plants in sandy soils benefit from frequent applications; those in heavy soils may not need as much. A soil test can help determine the particular balance of nitrogen, phosphorus, and potassium your garden needs. The staff of a local nursery can often recommend the fertilizer ratio and application rates for your area.

KINDS OF FERTILIZERS

Both organic and inorganic fertilizers are available in dry or liquid preparations. There's no difference between the elements in organic and inorganic fertilizers. Organic fertilizers, derived from plants and animals, act more slowly and require the action of microorganisms to break them down into the elements usable by the roots. Inorganic fertilizers are synthetic and act on the plant more quickly.

Dry fertilizers are worked into the ground and are spread to the roots by watering. Liquid fertilizers are added to water and usually applied to the roots. Foliar liquid fertilizers are sprayed onto the leaves where nutrients are absorbed.

Most rose gardeners rely on one of the "complete" dry rose fertilizers and supplemental applications of liquid fertilizer. The soil should be moist before adding a fertilizer; water again after applying to carry the nutrients to the roots. Do not spray fertilizer on foliage on hot (over 85°F) days. Whatever kind of fertilizer you use, always follow *exactly* the directions and proportions given on the product label. That a little is good doesn't mean a lot is better; excessive doses of fertilizer can severely harm a plant.

FREQUENCY OF APPLICATION

Species and shrub roses, old roses, and climbers usually need only one application of fertilizer in the early spring as the buds prepare to burst. Remontant types of old roses and climbers will benefit from a second feeding of liquid fertilizer after their first bloom.

Modern roses enjoy regular feeding to provide fuel for their growth and blooming. Begin fertilizing newly planted roses after the plants have become established, about 3 to 4 weeks after planting. Start fertilizing older plants after you have pruned and foliage starts to appear.

There are two schools of thought among gardeners regarding the frequency of subsequent applications. Some favor applications of fertilizer every 6 to 8 weeks three or four times during the growing season. Other gardeners swear by applications every 3 to 5 weeks, usually alternating dry and liquid fertilizers in reduced amounts. Fast-draining sandy soils benefit from the more frequent applications. You'll probably want to experiment and see which method works best for you.

In regions where winter temperatures drop below 10°F, stop feeding preparations including nitrogen to plants 6 weeks before the anticipated first frost and apply instead a fertilizer high in phosphorus and potassium to strengthen the plant for the winter.

INGREDIENTS IN A BALANCED PLANT DIET

Elements	Contributions	Signs of Malnutrition
Primary elements		
Nitrogen	Promotes green growth —good canes, stems, leaves. Used most heavily when the plant is growing most quickly.	Yellow leaves No new growth Failure of buds to open Small, pale flowers
Phosphorus	Good root growth and flower production	Dull green foliage Falling leaves Weak stems Abnormal root system Slow-to-open buds
Potassium	Vigorous growth	Yellow leaf margins, turning brown Weak stems Underdeveloped buds
Secondary elements		
Calcium	Growth of plant cells and good roots	Deformed growth and abnormal root development
Magnesium	Good growth	Mature yellow leaves, tinged maroon
Sulfur	Green growth	Yellowing of new leaves
Trace elements		
Boron	Good form	Small, curled, and scorched leaves Dead terminal buds
Chlorine	Good growth	Malformed foliage
Copper	Good growth	Poorly developed tips
Iron	Keeps plants green	Yellow foliage
Manganese	Increases nitrogen	Pale mottling of leaves
Molybdenum	Good growth	Poorly developed leaves
Zinc	Good growth	Malformed growth

IRON-DEFICIENCY CHLOROSIS

Chlorosis is an unnatural yellowing of foliage, with the veins usually remaining a darker green. It is caused by a shortage of iron available to the plant, which is a result of poor drainage, excess lime in the soil, or naturally alkaline soils. Proper preparation of the planting site based on results of a soil test is the best prevention.

Roses with some yellow or orange shadings in the petals are most susceptible to chlorosis. Spraying the leaves with a solution of chelated iron fertilizer will take care of mild cases. For severe cases improve the soil by working in iron chelate fertilizer around the plant according to the directions given on the package. Improve drainage or treat alkaline soil with soil sulfur according to package directions.

FERTILIZING ROSES IN CONTAINERS

Because roses grown in containers need more frequent watering and nutrients are thus leached from the soil at a faster rate, these plants need more frequent applications of fertilizer. Whether you're using dry or liquid fertilizer, a good rule of thumb is to halve the recommended dosage and apply it twice as often as directed by the label. As with plants in the ground, don't overfertilize. If you mistakenly apply too much, give the plant several thorough soakings of water to wash the excess out of the soil.

PESTS AND DISEASES

Take a leisurely walk through your garden every few days and enjoy the rewards of your labor. At the same time, keep your eyes open for early signs of trouble, such as wilted foliage, deformed flower buds, or spots on leaves.

If you discover any such warnings, don't jump to the conclusion that your garden is disease- or pest-ridden —unless, of course, you find some insects. Take time to diagnose the problem. Remember that many plant problems can be caused by a gardener's oversight or neglect. Not enough water can cause wilt; too much water can cause rot; alkaline soil can cause yellow leaves. Before spraying make sure the problem is not a cultural one. Symptoms, diagnoses, and methods of control of common insects and diseases attacking roses are listed in the chart on pages 42 and 43.

Top: Control aphids with regular applications of a pesticide spray, or use a systemic. Above: Discourage blackspot by keeping foliage dry and cleaning up debris.

PREVENTION IS THE KEY

A healthy and vigorous rose can withstand more injury from unwanted invaders than a rose that is under stress from lack of water or nutrients.

Buy high-quality plants that show no abnormal swellings on the roots or crowns and are free of discolored areas on the stems. Buy from reliable sources that guarantee their product to be disease-free. To further reduce the chance of disease, choose one of the many cultivars that have been shown to be particularly resistant to common rose diseases.

Some diseases can be prevented by watering correctly. Watering from above should be done only in the morning so the foliage has a chance to dry out before nightfall. Use a bubbler on the end of your hose when irrigating to prevent water from splattering soil or mulch on the leaves. Use of this technique slows the spread of powdery mildew and blackspot.

Perform maintenance pruning throughout the growing season. Remove all canes showing cankers as soon as you detect them, and destroy the prunings. Remove and destroy individual leaves bearing black spots as soon as you notice them.

Don't forget a winter cleanup. There will be fewer insects and disease organisms when the new leaves unfurl in the spring if you thoroughly clean all debris from the beds when your roses are dormant. To keep rust and blackspot from carrying over from year to year, strip all leaves from your bushes. Rake up any leaves that have fallen, and burn them or dump them in the garbage can. Spray the canes and twigs and the soil or mulch beneath with a specially formulated dormant spray.

Establish a regular spray schedule for disease and pest control during the growing season. You may never even see any evidence of pests or disease if you regularly take the time every two weeks or so to spray or dust the plants with a multipurpose pesticide. This program shouldn't take more than about an hour every 2 weeks for most rose gardens.

Systemics. An alternate approach to spraying is to use systemics. A *systemic* is a pesticide that is absorbed into the system of a plant, causing the plant to become toxic to insects. Systemics are often sold combined with nutrients so that one application serves a number of purposes.

There is no need for routine spraying to combat the normal attacks of aphids, spider mites, white flies, leaf-mining insects, leafhoppers, and other sucking types of pests if a systemic is applied every 6 weeks. The plant then has internal protection that cannot be washed off by rain or water from sprinklers.

Natural controls. The introduction of such predaceous insects as ladybug beetles, praying mantis, Trichogramma wasps, and lacewings can help keep the population of aphids and other pests under control. Remember, though, that if you do use chemical sprays or dusts, you may also kill these insects. Systemics will not harm these beneficial insects.

Birds can be a menace to the vegetable garden or fruit orchard, but they can be a delightful asset to the rose garden. Insect-eating species include bluebirds, chickadees, mockingbirds, orioles, robins, wrens, and warblers. You can encourage their visits by hanging bird feeders near the roses.

SYSTEMIC ROSE CARE

Spread the recommended amount of granules around the bush and work into the soil.

The nutrients and insecticides are dispensed systemically throughout the entire plant; even the new growth is protected against sucking insects as it develops.

USING CHEMICAL CONTROLS

There may be times, however, when you are faced with an invasion of pests overwhelming your usual methods of control. In such cases it's important to act quickly. Spray or dust at the very first sign of attack. Get the first aphids, the first brood of beetles, or the first invasion of thrips, and you'll be able to establish complete control much more quickly.

When you do use chemical controls, however, use them thoughtfully and carefully. Keep in mind the following guidelines for their safest, most effective use.

☐ Store all chemicals behind locked doors, in their original containers, with labels intact. Keep them away from food and out of the reach of children and pets.

☐ Observe all directions and precautions on pesticide labels. They are there for your benefit and safety.

☐ Use pesticides at the correct dosage and intervals as specified on the label to avoid unnecessary residues and injury to plants and animals. Never use a stronger spray than is recommended by the manufacturer. The sprays have been carefully formulated by experts to do the most effective job.

☐ Water plants thoroughly the day before spraying.

☐ Mix chemicals in an open area. Spray on calm days to prevent drifts. Work on the windward side when applying. Cover any nearby fishponds or birdbaths. Be fully clothed when spraying, and avoid prolonged inhalation of any chemical.

☐ Spray or dust both the tops *and* the undersides of the leaves. Insects and diseases most often work on the undersides of leaves.

☐ Dispose of surplus pesticides and used containers so as not to contaminate water or soil. Wrap in paper and place in the garbage can.

☐ After handling pesticides, be sure to wash up before you eat, drink, or smoke.

Some states have restrictions on the use of certain gardening chemicals. Check your state and local regulations if you have any doubts.

OTHER PESTS

Ants are often seen following the paths of aphids to eat the sticky honey residue. They may build nests in the ground, which can disturb the rose roots. Use a preparation containing diazinon to eradicate.

Deer love to feed on tender young rose shoots. Garden centers stock repellants that may deter deer, but high fences are the surest prevention.

Leafcutter bees cut perfect circles and ovals in rose leaves during the summer. There's no control for the leaf damage. Excise all wilted and dying shoots that result from the damage.

Moles can disturb roots with their tunneling when searching for food, causing unhealthy growth or even death in rose plants. Mole traps are available, or you can treat the soil with a soil insecticide containing diazinon. This will kill many of the soil insects on which moles feed.

Pine mice burrow underground and cut off roots. Watch for small exit holes and fast-flowing runoff. Place poisoned food inside the holes, and cover with pieces of tile or boards to protect other animals.

COMBATING PESTS AND DISEASES

Symptoms		Problems	Solutions
Clusters of tiny insects on young shoots, flower buds, or underside of leaves. Foliage and blooms stunted or deformed. Sticky honeydew left behind attracts ants.	Enlarged 2x	APHIDS. Soft-bodied green, brown, or reddish insects that suck plant juices.	Harmless lady beetles introduced into the garden will feed on aphids. Wipe out infestations with contact sprays such as Diazinon, Malathion, Sevin, and Orthene.
Foliage, flowers, and stems are chewed, devoured, or have holes drilled in them.	All life-size	BEETLES (including 1. Japanese, 2. rose chafer, 3. rose curculio, and 4. Fuller beetles). Their larvae also eat plant roots.	Pick off beetles by hand or knock them into a can of kerosene and water. Spray with Sevin, Diazinon, or Malathion.
Circular black spots with fringed margins appear on leaves. Leaves may turn yellow and drop prematurely. On more resistant varieties, leaves will remain green and hang onto bush.		BLACKSPOT. A fungus disease, easily spread to nearby bushes by rain or hose. Overwinters in small cane lesions or leaves left on ground.	Water with wand or soil soaker. If you must wet foliage, do it early in the day, so the bush can dry before night. Spray regularly with Funginex.
Flower buds eaten or leaves rolled and tied around the pest, eaten from inside. Most often a late spring problem.	Life-size	BUDWORM AND OTHER CATERPILLARS. Larvae of moths and butterflies that feed on rose foliage.	Cut out infested buds and leaves. Apply Diazinon, Sevin, or Orthene.
Holes eaten into leaves from the underside, causing a skeletonized glazed effect. Appear early in the spring. Later, large holes eaten in leaves and, finally, the veins are devoured.	Approx. life-size	BRISTLY ROSE SLUGS (often called cane borers or leafworms). Half-inch long, hairy, slimy larvae of sawfly. Young eat underside of leaves; adults eat entire leaf.	Act quickly to stop their speedy damage. Spray with Sevin.
Lesions in the woody tissue of a cane, poor growth, or death above the affected area.		CANKER. A disease caused by parasitic fungus that usually enters plant through wounds or dying tissue.	Prune out and burn all affected areas, cutting well below canker with shears dipped in alcohol after each cut. Paint with pruning paint or spray. Spray regularly with Captan.
Roundish, rough-surfaced growths near plant's crown or on roots. Plants lose vigor, produce abnormal flowers and foliage, and eventually die.		CROWN GALL. Soil-borne bacterial disease, which can live on in soil after affected plant is removed and may or may not affect a new plant.	Do not buy plants with swellings near bud union or on roots. Remove and burn infected parts, seal with pruning paint. Or remove entire bush and treat soil with all-purpose fumigant before setting new plants.
Top surface of leaves turns pale and becomes covered with tiny yellow specks similar to damage of spider mites.	Life-size Enlarged 3x	LEAFHOPPERS. Tiny, greenish yellow, jumping insects found on underside of leaves. They suck out contents of leaf cells.	Apply Orthene, Diazinon or Malathion.
Pale green foliage and stunted growth in spite of good gardening practices. Root examination reveals abnormal swelling, knotty enlargements with tiny white eggs inside, discolored lesions, or dead tissue.	Enlarged approx. 5x Eggs	NEMATODES. Disease caused by tiny animal pests that invade the roots of the plant.	Check with your County Agent or Agricultural Experiment Station for help in diagnosis and control. All-purpose soil fumigants or nematocides are beneficial.

Symptoms		Problems	Solutions
Holes in cut ends of canes or punctures in stems. Wilting of plant shoot, foliage, and canes. Sometimes slight swelling of canes.		PITHBORERS (including 1. rose stem sawfly, 2. rose stem girdler, and 3. small carpenter bees). Pests bore into cane and lay eggs. Larvae eat through canes.	Cut out canes below infested portion during spring pruning. Seal exposed tips with pruning paint.
White powdery masses of spores on young leaves, shoots, and buds; distorted young shoots; stunted foliage.		POWDERY MILDEW. Disease spread by wind. Encouraged by warm days followed by cool nights. Overwinters on fallen leaves and inside stems and bud scales.	Apply Funginex. For best results, apply when mildew is first noticed.
Large mossy or callus swellings on stems or roots. Look like crown gall, but if cut open, you'll find larvae. (Mostly on species roses.)		ROSE GALL (including mossy rose gall and rose root gall). Caused by wasplike insects that bore into canes and lay eggs. The growing larvae cause swelling.	Insecticides do not control. Prune infested stems and burn to destroy larvae before they emerge. Seal exposed area.
Black, deformed flower buds and leaves that die prematurely.	Enlarged 3x	ROSE MIDGE. Tiny yellowish flies lay eggs in growing tips of stems. Hatching maggots destroy tender tissue.	Remove and destroy affected areas. Spray with Orthene.
Wilting and darkening of foliage, which drops prematurely. Close examination reveals mature stems encrusted with hard-shelled insects.	Approx. life-size	ROSE SCALES. Round, dirty white, gray, or brown shell-covered insects that suck sap from plants.	Prune out and destroy old, infested wood. Apply Malathion, Sevin, Orthene, or Dormant Oil Spray.
Wilted leaves that may drop. Yellow dots and light green mottling appear on upper leaf surface opposite pustules of powdery, rust-colored spores on the lower surface.		RUST. Overwinters in fallen leaves, spread by wind. The disease is especially troublesome along the Pacific Coast.	Remove and destroy all rusted leaves during pruning. Spray with Funginex. Select rust-resistant varieties when planting new roses.
Stippled leaves appear dry, turn brown, red, yellow, or gray, then curl and drop off. Sometimes webs are visible on the underside of leaves.		SPIDER MITES. Minute pests that suck juices from underside of rose foliage. Abundant in hot, dry weather.	Clean up trash and weeds in early spring to destroy breeding places. Spray infestations with Diazinon, Orthene, Malathion, or Dormant Oil Spray.
Flecked petals and deformed flowers, especially on white varieties.		THRIPS. Very active, tiny, slender, brownish yellow, winged insects that hide in base of infected flowers.	Cut off and dispose of spent blooms. Apply Diazinon, Malathion, or Orthene.
Small, angular, colorless spots on foliage. Ring, oakleaf, watermark, or mosaic patterns develop on leaves.		VIRUS DISEASES (including mosaic). Spread by propagation of infected plants.	Prevention is only control. Do not buy any plants exhibiting the symptoms described. Dispose of entire affected plants to prevent spread of virus to other nearby plants.

PROTECTION FROM THE ELEMENTS

Most roses are pretty resilient plants ("glorified brambles," as one cranky rosarian observed), but many do need some protection from extreme fluctuations in temperature and the drying effects of wind. *All* roses will bless you with their best flowers and prove a credit to your garden if you pamper them a little.

WIND

Any strong, constant wind is bad for roses. Wind hastens the evaporation of moisture from the leaves and in extreme cases, even if the soil is damp, the plant becomes severely dehydrated because it is unable to draw enough moisture from the roots fast enough to replenish the foliage. A hedge of more resilient protective shrubs or a fence can sometimes help shield the roses.

A hot and dry wind is particularly troublesome to roses. A fence will likely not be enough protection in this situation. Air on the leeward side of a fence is more turbulent than on the leeward side of a hedge. And most important, a fence doesn't add moisture to dry air as a screen of shrubs or trees will.

Allow at least 10 feet between rosebushes and a screen or hedge. Select deep-rooted shrubs that grow well in your climate and form a solid screen.

HEAT

Very hot weather fatigues a rose plant. At temperatures above 90°F, the plant uses food faster than its foliage can manufacture it from sunlight, water, and nutrients. If you live in a hot climate, be careful not to overprune your roses. During the winter prune only enough to shape the plants. The less-severe pruning will allow a greater abundance of foliage to develop to provide the plant with a storehouse of energy before the hot summer months. Rose gardeners in cooler climates need not be so restrained.

In extremely hot, sunny areas you might add a lath covering over part of the rose garden to give some shade during the hottest part of the day. Roses in containers should be moved to partially shaded locations.

Cool nights or dark, damp days can cause *balling*, a situation in which blooms open halfway and then stop. Cut off such blooms when they start to ball to allow for better growth when weather conditions improve. If you live in a cool or foggy summer area, you might select rose varieties with fewer petals, which will reduce balling.

Sometimes, after very mild or warm winters, branch tips may remain bare or the side buds on some canes will fail to grow because they were not chilled enough to induce normal growth. Prune out such canes.

FREEZING

The question of protection from freezing is probably the most controversial in rose culture. Some experts go so far as to advise against any winter protection for roses, except a deep layer of mulch, even in very harsh climates. On the other side, some people in the same area recommend tipping and burying the entire plant. You'll probably want to talk with neighbors or friends or members of your local rose society to find out what methods provide sufficient protection in your area.

PARTIAL COVERING

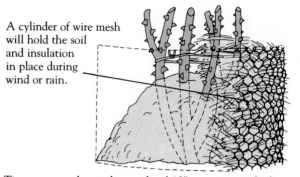

A cylinder of wire mesh will hold the soil and insulation in place during wind or rain.

Tie canes together and mound soil 12″ or more over bud union. Leave exposed until soil freezes, then cover with evergreen boughs or straw to keep mound frozen.

COMPLETE COVERING

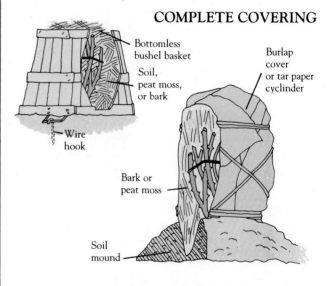

Bottomless bushel basket

Soil, peat moss, or bark

Wire hook

Burlap cover or tar paper cyclinder

Bark or peat moss

Soil mound

Many roses, including quite a few species, shrubs, old roses, and climbers, are naturally cold hardy and need little or no protection. A number of newer hybrid teas are marketed as subzero plants needing only minimal protection. Miniature roses are more cold-resistant than most hybrid teas or other garden roses and require little winter protection. In warm climates they even continue blooming all year.

One of a plant's best defenses against cold weather is proper summer care. Vigorous bushes are able to withstand cold far better than unhealthy ones. Roses planted in locations that are protected by trees, large shrubs, or structures need less artificial defense than bushes exposed to the elements.

Sudden changes in temperature in the fall, before the plant has hardened off for winter, can be disastrous. Early freezes kill more canes than much colder winter freezes. To discourage new growth that can be destroyed by an early freeze, avoid late summer feedings of nitrogen and hold back on water.

In areas where temperatures drop to 10°–15°F for as long as 2 weeks at a time, most bush roses can be adequately protected by mounding the base of each plant with fresh, loose soil or compost that drains well. After the first hard

COMPLETE WINTER PROTECTION FOR TREE ROSES

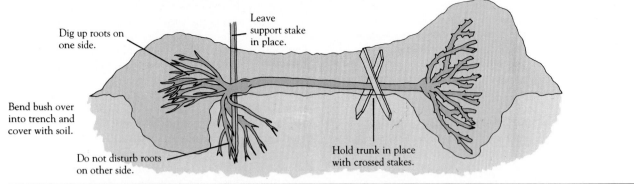

Dig up roots on one side.

Leave support stake in place.

Bend bush over into trench and cover with soil.

Do not disturb roots on other side.

Hold trunk in place with crossed stakes.

COMPLETE WINTER PROTECTION FOR CLIMBING ROSES

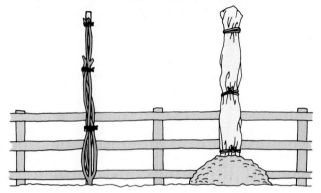

1. Attach a sturdy pole to the fence or trellis above the climber's crown.
2. Untie the canes from the fence or trellis and retie them securely to the pole.
3. Wrap the tied canes in straw or evergreen boughs and burlap, then pile soil a foot or so deep over the crown.

1. Arch canes near the crown so they don't break, marking location of buried rose with stakes.
2. Hold the canes in place with crossed stakes, being careful not to damage the roots with marking stakes.
3. Cover all canes with 3″ or 4″ of soil.

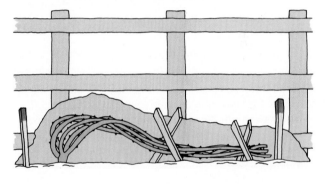

frost, mound up soil to a depth of 6–8 inches around the plants. Most gardeners use soil from another area of the garden for mounding to avoid disturbing the roots. Prune the height of each plant only enough to prevent the plant from whipping about in the wind or to fit under protective covering, and dispose of the clippings. Spray the plant with an antidesiccant dormant spray, and then add 8–10 inches of leaves, straw, or other mulch throughout the bed, securing it with chicken wire or some other netting.

"Rose caps" are available from garden suppliers, or you can devise your own cover from the examples we have illustrated. Prune the plants to fit under whatever cover you use; they may look scrawny the next spring but will regain their form by summer.

Where temperatures dip below zero, additional protection, such as completely burying the plant under soil, may be required.

Try not to be too eager to remove winter coverings in the spring. The tender growth underneath can be easily killed by even a light freeze. Keep some straw or mulch handy to cover plants in the event of a late frost.

Roses in containers. When the temperature falls below 28°F, place the plant in an unheated shelter away from frost and chilling winds. Even in this shelter the temperature

should not fall below 10°F. When the bush begins to defoliate, remove all the foliage. Water occasionally during dormancy, just so the soil doesn't completely dry out. Do not feed. After the danger of frost is over, move the pot outdoors. Prune lightly to initiate new growth (see pages 46–49).

In mild areas where the temperature stays above 28°F, the plant can live outdoors all year. Cut back its water and eliminate feeding during winter months to induce dormancy.

Tree roses. In mild-winter areas, wrap the plants in straw and cover with burlap. No protection is necessary in warm-winter areas.

If temperatures fall as low as 10°F, in late fall dig under the roots on one side until the plant can be pulled over on the ground without breaking root connections with the soil. Stake the plant to the ground and cover the entire plant with 4–5 inches of soil. In spring, after the soil thaws and frost danger is past, remove the soil and set the plant upright once again.

Climbing roses. A burlap wrapping is adequate protection for climbing roses in mild-winter climates. But in areas with hard freezes, you can bury climbers the same way you do tree roses.

PRUNING

A rose left unpruned can grow into a mass of tangled brambles that produces small or inferior blooms. Proper pruning removes nonproductive or damaged wood and leaves a few good canes as the foundation of a healthy bush producing well-formed flowers. Pruning allows you to create an attractive shape and desired size that fits into your landscape.

TIMING

Prune modern roses just before the rosebush breaks dormancy after the last frost. The right time can fall anytime between January in warm areas and April in severe winter climates.

Old roses bear their flowers on wood produced the previous year, so they should be pruned only after they have bloomed.

EQUIPMENT

As an act of kindness both to your plants and to yourself, use *sharp*, clean, well-lubricated tools for pruning. For regular-size roses, you'll need three types of cutting instruments.

☐ A fine-toothed, curved saw for cutting woody tissue
☐ Hand pruning shears
☐ Long-handled lopping shears for thick canes or getting into hard-to-reach places

In addition, a pair of heavy-duty leather garden gloves will thwart thorns and protect your hands.

To prune miniature roses, you'll need only a pair of hand pruners for thick stems and a smaller, more delicate pair of shears for trimming.

ANGLE TO CUT

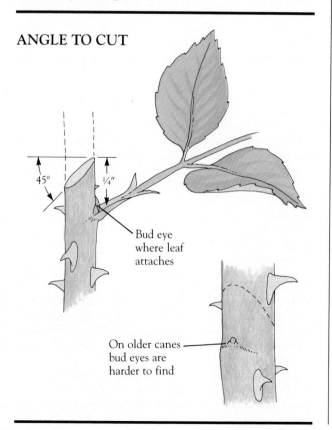

45°   ¼"

Bud eye where leaf attaches

On older canes bud eyes are harder to find

MAKING CUTS

Cut at sharp, 30–45-degree angles. Make all cuts down to a cane, to the base of the cane above the bud union, or to a strong outside bud or bud eye on stem nodes. A *bud eye* is a small bulge with a tiny "eye" and a horizontal crease below. After dormancy or if stimulated by pruning, the bud eye will develop into a new shoot.

Notice the direction in which the bud or bud eye is pointing. Because the bud is the origin of all new replacement growth, it should be directed from the interior of the plant so as not to create a tangle of canes competing for sunlight in the center. Make cuts about ¼ inch above the bud. If cuts are made too high above the bud, the wood above the bud will die, providing a haven for pests and diseases.

When using pruning shears, make sure the cutting blade is on the lower side to ensure a clean cut. The slight injury that results from pressure on the noncutting side should be on the top part of the cane that will be discarded.

HOW MUCH TO PRUNE

Whatever kind of rose you're pruning, always cut away deadwood. It's not going to come back to life, it's unattractive, and it harbors diseases. You can then make intelligent decisions about shaping your plant.

Pruning while the plant is dormant removes buds without reducing the energy stored in roots and branches. The heavier the pruning, the more buds are removed, and the more energy will be available to each remaining bud.

About all that gardeners in severe climates need to do is cut back wood that has been killed over winter. For those in more moderate and warm climates, there are three basic types of pruning.

☐ Prune weak plants heavily to stimulate vigorous growth. Strongly growing plants can handle more buds and still grow vigorously.
☐ If you wish large, showy roses for cut flowers, prune more heavily. Each bud will grow more vigorously and produce a larger rose.
☐ Prune most rose plants in your landscape moderately so that you will have smaller but numerous flowers on a more attractive shrub.

Severe or heavy. The plant is cut back to three or four canes, 6–10 inches high. This method is used to produce a few very showy blooms.

Moderate. Five to twelve canes are left, about 18–24 inches high. Moderate pruning develops a much larger bush than severe pruning and is best suited to most garden roses.

Light. In this method less than one-third of the plant is cut back. Light pruning produces a profusion of short-stemmed flowers on larger bushes. This method is practiced mainly with floribundas, grandifloras, first-year hybrid teas, and species roses.

All three methods can be used by different gardeners within the same climatic zone. It's a matter of preference through experience. It usually takes several years to learn the best pruning method for each variety of rose. You may discover that a light pruning works best on a regular basis, with a heavy pruning every 4 or 5 years. If you cut back too far one year, you'll know to go easier the next.

PRUNING BUSH ROSES

It is easier to prune bush roses if the bud union is above ground. If you have planted it below the soil level, you might wish to remove soil from around the bud union while you prune so you can see the origin of all the canes.

First, remove any deadwood down to the nearest healthy, dormant bud eye. Make the cut at least 1 inch below the dead area. If no live buds remain, remove the entire branch or cane to the bud union.

Examine the plant carefully for canker or other diseased areas (see page 42). Cut down to a plump bud at least 1 inch below any evidence of disease. Although canes may look green and healthy, check the top of each cane to make sure the pith in the center is creamy white, not brown or gray. Prune down to above a bud where the pith is healthy or to the bud union if the pith is diseased all the way down.

Cut out weak, spindly, and deformed growth. This includes canes that grow straight out, then curve upward (called doglegs). Remove canes growing toward the center of the bush. If two branches cross, remove the weaker one.

Remove old canes. Old canes are thick and woody, and produce a profusion of twigs rather than strong stems.

Remove all suckers or reversion growth (undesired shoots that come from the rootstock below the bud union). Sucker foliage is different in color and form from the foliage of the rest of the plant. If you do not remove suckers, they will soon be dominant. When cutting them out, take all the sucker base from the crown area along with a piece of the crown if necessary.

Next, thin out the remaining healthy canes to the shape you want and cut them back to the height you want. After severe winters all the canes may have to be cut to within several inches of the bud union. In such cases you can't worry about shape; just save as much live wood as you can.

1. Pruning will rejuvenate this overgrown rose bush.
2. To open up bush, remove old canes with lopping shears.

3. Sharp hand-pruning shears handle small canes and twigs.
4. A pruning saw simplifies removal of woody growth.

5. Pruning paint protects tender cut canes from disease.
Severe pruning produces fewer but showier blossoms.

Moderate pruning—here, to 9 canes—ensures good foliage and bloom production for an impressive display.

PRUNING CLIMBING ROSES

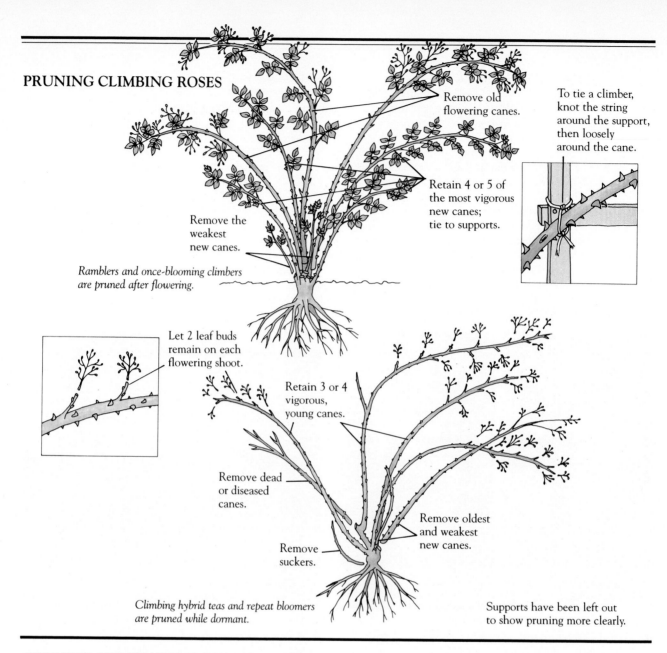

Remove old flowering canes.

To tie a climber, knot the string around the support, then loosely around the cane.

Retain 4 or 5 of the most vigorous new canes; tie to supports.

Remove the weakest new canes.

Ramblers and once-blooming climbers are pruned after flowering.

Let 2 leaf buds remain on each flowering shoot.

Retain 3 or 4 vigorous, young canes.

Remove dead or diseased canes.

Remove oldest and weakest new canes.

Remove suckers.

Climbing hybrid teas and repeat bloomers are pruned while dormant.

Supports have been left out to show pruning more clearly.

PRUNING AND TRAINING CLIMBING ROSES

Don't prune any climbers (except to cut out deadwood) for the first 2 or 3 years. This will allow them to establish mature canes. Climbers that bloom only once should be pruned after they have bloomed; climbing hybrid teas and continuous-blooming climbers are pruned in early spring while dormant.

Prune ramblers and other once-blooming climbers soon after flowering. Cut out diseased or dead canes and remove older, gray canes as well as weak new ones. Most climber canes are good for only two or three seasons. Save the green, healthy canes. Cut the laterals on which the flowers appear back to four or five buds to shape the plant as desired. Be sure to remove any suckers from the base of the plant.

Some of the less-vigorous climbers need to be trimmed each spring to remove winterkill and twiggy growth. Later, after blooming is over, remove the faded flowers.

Hybrid climbers and everblooming large-flowered climbers are pruned while dormant. Do not take as much wood from the everbloomers as you do from the hybrids. Proceed as you would with bush roses: Remove dead and

diseased canes; get rid of sucker growth; remove old or weak new growth. Retain three or four vigorous young canes.

Keep flowers plucked off everblooming roses, but do not take foliage, since the repeat blooms are produced from the top leaves immediately under the old flower cluster. When removing hybrid blooms, leave two leaf buds on each flowering shoot.

All climbers are pruned to make them fit the place where they are being trained—arbors, fences, pergolas, pillars, or trellises. Train them by letting the canes grow long and then arching or tying them in a horizontal position with the tips of the canes pointed downward. This will stimulate the lateral buds to produce a flowering branch instead of concentrating growth in the terminal bud. See the diagram for directions on how to tie the canes.

Shortening some of the long upright canes will stimulate laterals to develop and continue to elongate and cover the support.

Ramblers and other climbers can be *pegged down,* or their tips anchored to the ground, to produce massive plants that can cover large areas.

PRUNING TREE ROSES

Standards are pruned in the same way as shrub roses. Cut out dead or diseased branches or canes, leaving healthy canes pruned back to a good bud or bud eye. Keep the shape as symmetrical as possible so the foliage will fill out full and round. Suckers can grow from the rootstock or from the trunk stock. Cut them as close to their base as possible.

PRUNING OLD, SHRUB, AND SPECIES ROSES

Most old, shrub, and species roses need only a light trimming to shape them and remove deadwood. As before, those that bloom once a year should be pruned after blooming; others, in winter or early spring. A brief rundown on the requirements for old roses is presented at right. Shrub and species roses need very little pruning, and part of their charm is their natural growth habit. Remove spent blooms.

PRUNING OLD GARDEN ROSES

☐ **Gallica**. Remove twiggy growth after flowers bloom. Shape lightly during winter if desired.

☐ **Damask**. Remove twiggy growth after flowering; cut back lateral shoots to three buds. Main canes can be cut back to increase bushiness.

☐ **Alba**. Remove twiggy growth and cut back most recent growth by one-third after flowering.

☐ **Centifolia and Moss**. Reduce canes and side shoots after blooming by one-third to produce a bushier plant.

☐ **China**. Prune lightly by cutting side shoots back about one-third during the winter.

☐ **Bourbon and Portland**. Cut back the main canes by one-third and side shoots to three buds in winter. Trim twiggy growth after blooming.

☐ **Tea**. Prune lightly as you would a hybrid tea bush.

☐ **Hybrid Perpetual**. After the plants bloom, cut back the main shoots by one-third and shorten side shoots.

PRUNING MINIATURE ROSES

Prune miniatures as you would a bush rose, but lightly. Very vigorous varieties grown out of doors in warm climates may need heavier pruning to maintain their compactness. Some of the very small miniatures (sometimes called "micro-minis") may need no pruning at all.

YEAR-ROUND CARE

Prune and groom your roses as they grow. Cut out weak and spindly shoots, suckers, and obvious signs of disease. Remove flowers as soon as they have passed their peak.

Flowers of hybrid teas are produced in waves. Allowing the plant to set seeds increases the interval between periods of bloom. During the first growing season of a newly planted rose, just snip the flowers; a young plant needs all the leaves it can produce. When you remove fading flowers during subsequent growing seasons, don't just snip off the flower. Instead, cut back to a five-leaflet leaf. Cuts at these major leaves result in stronger shoots as the plant continues to develop. In cold-winter areas, allow hips to form after the final wave of bloom. Formation of hips slows down growth and hardens the plant for winter.

Rosarians who want to produce large blooms for shows disbud most of the side foliage and flower buds and allow only one or a selected few terminal buds to mature.

PRUNING TREE ROSES

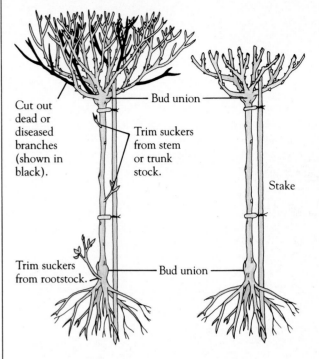

Cut out dead or diseased branches (shown in black).

Bud union

Trim suckers from stem or trunk stock.

Stake

Trim suckers from rootstock.

Bud union

CUTTING

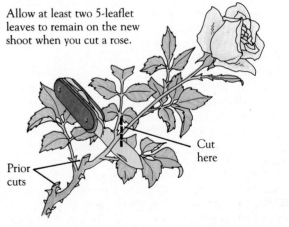

Allow at least two 5-leaflet leaves to remain on the new shoot when you cut a rose.

Cut here

Prior cuts

DISBUDDING

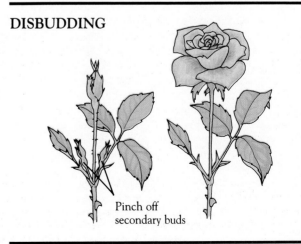

Pinch off secondary buds

PROPAGATION

Starting new plants from existing plants is fairly easy. Duplicating roses that you already grow saves money, and it's a great experience to watch the new plant emerge and develop. You can share with friends or exchange cuttings or seedlings with other rosarians in order to build a collection of hard-to-find roses. Just be sure that any plants you reproduce are nonpatented roses (see page 16).

But perhaps the most fun is to create a new rose from plants in your own or a friend's garden through hybridizing. You can do this scientifically with a certain rose in mind, or you can see what you come up with by just taking a chance on the roll of the genetic dice.

SEXUAL REPRODUCTION

Hybridizing. All roses are bisexual. Nature has provided each rose with both stamens (male organs) and pistils (female organs) for pollination. Roses are hybridized by taking the pollen from the stamens on the flower of one plant and applying it to the pistils on the flower of another. Plants grown from the seeds resulting from this cross will be the offspring of the two plants. The process begins early in the rose season to allow plenty of time for the complete cycle to take place before dormancy sets in again.

Whether a plant serves as the male or female parent appears to make no difference in its ability to pass on its characteristics to the offspring. Breeders usually make reciprocal crossings, using the same variety as both male and female.

Early in the year choose the cultivars you wish to pollinate. Then select a blossom on each plant that is less than half open. Leaving the flowers on the plants, carefully remove the flower petals from both flowers, and you will find both sets of reproductive organs. The very center contains the pistils, delicate stalks connected to an ovary at the bottom end and a pollen-receiving stigma at the tip.

Surrounding the pistils are the stamens, slender stalks tipped by the anthers—kernel-like sacs that hold the pollen. The first phase of hybridization is to emasculate both parents. Even if a particular rose is being used as a female, the anthers must be removed before they have a chance to open and self-pollinate the rose. Pluck the anthers off with tweezers or cut them with a sharp knife, being careful not to damage the pistils.

Place the anthers gathered from the rose chosen to be the male to dry in a closed jar, dated and identified according to variety. The flower that furnished the pollen may be cut off the plant and discarded (or used as a female in a simultaneous experiment). Cover the female flower with a paper bag so it cannot be fertilized by pollen carried by the wind.

In a day or so the anthers inside the jar will ripen and open, releasing their dustlike pollen grains. These minute capsules contain the sperm. During this time the female parent prepares to receive the pollen. When the female's stigmas are tipped with a sticky secretion, it is time for the pollination.

Brush all the dry pollen onto the receptive stigmas with an artist's camel's hair brush. The secretion of the stigma not only makes the pollen adhere but also dissolves the capsule, releasing the tiny sperm. The sperm then send down tiny, hairlike pollen tubes through the stalks to an

1. Remove outer petals of selected parents to expose reproductive organs. *2.* Pollen-bearing anthers tip stamens, which surround the pistils in center.

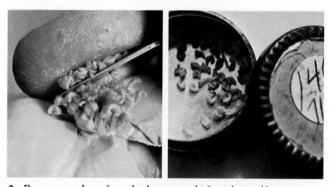

3. Remove anthers from both parents before they self-pollinate rose. *4.* Store anthers from selected male parent inside labeled container and allow to dry.

5. Sticky secretion on tips of stigmas indicates that female is pollen receptive. *6.* Anthers release dustlike pollen grains containing sperm at about the same time.

7. Use small, soft brush to place dried pollen on female's stigmas. *8.* Protect pollinated bud from dust and unwanted pollen with glassine bag, and label bud.

9. *If pollination is successful, as in hip at right, hip swells with growth.* **10.** *Seeds, sometimes borne on outside of hip, can be harvested about 2½ months after the cross.*

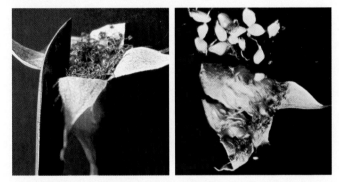

11. *Cut hip carefully with small, sharp knife after it has matured and turned color.* **12.** *To reveal the seeds, divide hip into sections and peel them open.*

13. *Stratify seeds by storing in peat moss at 40°F for up to 6 weeks.* **14.** *Plant seeds in a loose growing medium or allow to germinate. This seedling is 1 week old.*

15. *Evaluate results in about 2 months; weed out weak or poor-colored seedlings.* **16.** *Label promising seedlings for continued development and budding at summer's end.*

ovule containing unfertilized eggs. There, a male reproductive cell seeks out and unites with an egg.

After the crossing is complete, label the female flower to identify the variety that served as the male parent. Tie the bag again over the flower to protect it from dust or unwanted pollen. Now it's up to nature. Don't be disappointed by a failure. The percentage of fertilizations is low.

The hip will dry up and fall off the plant if the pollination fails to take. If the pollination is successful, the hip will stay green and within a few weeks will swell with growth. Hips ripen in about 2½ months, turning bright orange, yellow, red, or brown, depending on the variety. Gather the hips (along with the label) when they first turn color, before they become overripe. Fresh seeds germinate faster.

Next, slice the hip carefully with a knife, expose the seeds, and remove them. There may be only 1 seed or as many as 50. Condition the seeds by storing them in plastic bags of peat moss. Refrigerate them at 40°F for about 6 weeks. When you remove the seeds from refrigeration, plant them as outlined in the next section.

The first flowers may appear 7 to 8 weeks after germination. This is the first indication of your results. Now you must make the decision, according to your personal preference, whether the seedling merits being allowed to develop or if it should be discarded.

If you keep the seedling, you can either let it grow on its own roots or bud it onto a vigorous rootstock (see page 52).

Growing from seed. Don't expect to produce a rose identical to a hybrid from its seed. Even if the plant self-fertilizes, the seed will not reproduce "true", but will revert to some combination of characteristics of its parents.

Seed propagation can be used with self-fertilized species roses or with the seeds resulting from hybridization.

Select a shallow tray or flat with several drainage holes and fill it with fine sand or vermiculite. Remove the seeds from the hip and plant them ½ inch deep. Water thoroughly. Keep the growing medium moist (not soggy) and warm (around 55°–60°F). Provide no light for the first month. Then give the tray 16 hours of light a day.

Germination will soon begin and continue for 2 or 3 months. Seedlings emerge with a bent neck and straighten out in a few days. When the cotyledons (seed leaves) stretch out horizontally and turn green, they are then ready to transplant to a potting medium. The American Rose Society recommends a medium composed of equal parts of sterilized topsoil, perlite, and peat moss. To each quart of the mixture add 1 ounce of dolomite lime, 1 ounce of superphosphate, 1 ounce rose food, and 1 ounce of 50 percent captan.

Transplant the tiny seedlings into well-drained, large, plastic or metal pans or flats filled with the potting medium. Give them 16 hours of good light per day in a warm place (70°F). Fluorescent fixtures give excellent, controlled lighting for growing the seedlings.

Water sparingly and blot off any water that remains on leaves. Give the seedlings plenty of air circulation. After the first true leaves form, transplant the seedlings again into 3-inch pots with the same soil mixture, continue growing in flats, or transplant them into the garden. Seedlings may bloom when they are around 2 months old.

VEGETATIVE REPRODUCTION

Plants propagated by stem cuttings or budding will be identical to the plant from which the cutting or bud is taken. Cuttings can be made from hardwood that is one season old or from softwood that is just a few months old.

Modern roses do not grow well on their own roots, so budding is the best way to propagate them.

MAKING SOFTWOOD STEM CUTTINGS

Let the top two 5-leaflet leaves remain; pull off lower leaves, being careful not to damage buds. Dip in root hormone stimulant.

Set cuttings into damp soil mix.

Seal in a plastic bag until new shoots appear—about 5 to 8 weeks.

Hardwood cuttings. Use hardwood cuttings to propagate old roses and climbing roses.

In late fall or early winter cut mature canes of the current season's growth into 5–6-inch lengths. Bury them vertically in a box of sand or peat moss and store them in a cool, dark place (32°–50°F). Keep the sand or peat moss moist through winter. The plants should be ready to put out into the garden in spring.

If you live in a warm-winter climate, it may be difficult for you to find a cool enough place to store your cuttings. But you need look no farther than your refrigerator. Wrap the cuttings in plastic and leave them in the refrigerator for 2 or 3 weeks. Then pot them in sand and perlite, peat moss, or a soil-less medium; and put the whole pot inside a plastic bag. Place in the refrigerator again for 2 or 3 months. Then remove the bag and place the pot in filtered sunlight and begin watering.

Softwood stem cuttings. These cuttings are an easy way to reproduce favorite old and shrub roses.

Make 6–8-inch cuttings when bloom has faded. Remove the flower, along with a few inches of the top stem. Leave only one or two leaves at the top of the cutting. Dip the bottom end of the cutting into a root hormone stimulant to speed up root development.

Set cuttings to one-half their length into a damp growing medium composed of equal parts sand (or perlite) and peat moss (or vermiculite).

Insert two tall stakes into the soil to support a plastic bag. Place the pot in the bag and seal to create a greenhouselike climate. Store in a bright place away from direct sunlight.

Remove the bag when new growth begins (usually after 5 to 8 weeks). Transplant cutting to a pot or a spot in the garden where it will get partial shade for a couple of weeks.

Budding. Budding is the common propagation method used for hybrid roses to give them a more vigorous root system. The technique is an inexpensive way of duplicating plants, since each cane cutting (budwood) will have at least four buds, each capable of producing a new plant on individual rootstocks.

In the fall or winter select a healthy piece of rootstock and root 8- to 10-inch-long cuttings, one to a 10-inch pot, leaving only the top two buds to develop. *Rosa multiflora* and 'Dr. Huey' are the most commonly used plants; any sturdy shrub or old rose that roots easily will do. A sucker growing from below the bud union of an established plant is ideal.

The following spring or summer, cut a piece of budwood 6–8 inches long from a stem of a rose that has just finished blooming. Using a small, sharp knife, cut a *scion* (a single bud and a small portion of the surrounding bark) from the budwood.

Then cut a shallow T-shaped opening in the outer skin just above the soil on the cane of the rooted stock. Insert the bud or scion into the T-cut on the rootstock plant. Be sure that the bud is all the way into the cut.

Bind the bud into the grafting cut with a budding rubber or a length of plastic gardening tape. The bud will develop a few weeks later in the season; remove the binding around it when it does. In the late winter following, cut off the rootstock just above the bud and let the plant grow from the new bud. Transplant into the ground in the fall.

GROWING MINIATURE ROSES INDOORS

Miniature roses will bloom indoors all year, except for about 2 months' rest. You can expect a cycle of blooms every 6 to 8 weeks. With roses potted up at various times, it's possible to have a continual flowering display. Select compact, low-growing varieties for indoor use.

Plant miniatures in a 4–8-inch pot with a mixture of equal parts sterilized garden soil, peat moss (or other organic humus), and coarse sand (or perlite). Be sure the container has excellent drainage. Soak the freshly planted rose in water almost up to the rim of the pot until all bubbling stops.

After planting and soaking, put the plant on a cool porch, in a cold frame, or in a cool, protected outdoor area where it can acclimate itself for 2 to 4 weeks. When renewed growth begins, bring the plant indoors and place it in a sunny window.

Keep the soil evenly moist, never soggy wet. Occasionally let the surface dry; then water well from the top of the pot. Yellow leaves indicate inadequate drainage or too much water.

Yellow leaves can also indicate that the surrounding air is too dry. Miniature roses like more moisture than the average house provides. You can increase humidity by keeping the plant on a tray filled with pebbles or sand. Maintain some water in the bottom of the tray but not enough to reach the bottom of the pot. Routine washing of the foliage in the sink will help add moisture, remove any residues from sprays or household grease, and keep the insect population under control.

Feed with a houseplant fertilizer monthly and follow a preventive spray program, as for regular outdoor roses, to control diseases and pests. (See pages 40–42.) The worst enemy of miniature roses is spider mite. Keep your eyes open and provide early treatment.

Some growers of miniature roses suggest an annual 8-weeks' rest for plants during the hottest summer months. Place the plant in the vegetable crisper of the refrigerator. After the forced dormancy, cut the plant back to one-half its size and resume normal care. Or you can give your indoor minis a fall rest by leaving them outside for a couple of months; bring them inside by the middle of December. Protect them from frost by placing them along a wall outside a heated room and cover them with straw. Prune before bringing plants back inside.

Prune the plant anytime it's necessary to keep it to the desired shape and size. Cut back about one-third its height with sharp, clean shears, just above a five-leaflet leaf. Pinch or trim new shoots to encourage branching. Keep spent blooms pinched off. You may need to repot each year when you repot other plants grown indoors.

USING ARTIFICIAL LIGHT

Miniature roses are good candidates for light gardening. The plants remain compact, since they never have to reach for the light source, and they're covered with blooms most of the year, in cycles of six to eight weeks.

Place the plants under a light fixture that will provide 20 watts of light per square foot. Keep the light source 10–12 inches above the top of the rose. Set the lights on a timer to establish a routine of 16–18 hours of light per day.

You can choose from a wide variety of lighting fixtures and bulbs. Many people favor the old reliable formula of equal light from fluorescent tubes and incandescent bulbs. You may elect to use two cool-white fluorescent tubes, one cool and one warm tube, or the full-spectrum fluorescents that are designed for plant growth, such as Agrolite, Vitelite, or Duro-lite.

Miniature roses, from left to right: 'Cupcake', 'Green Ice', 'Judy Fischer', 'Starina', 'Over the Rainbow', 'Green Ice'.

Enjoying Roses Indoors

THE BEAUTY OF ROSES ISN'T LIMITED TO THE GARDEN. ᔥ CUT FLOWERS BRIGHTEN ANY DECOR WITH COLOR AND FRAGRANCE; OR PRESERVE YOUR ROSES BY CREATING A POTPOURRI.

The charm, beauty, and fragrance of roses need not be confined to the garden during the growing season. Cut flowers can brighten a dim corner of a room or serve as a centerpiece for a party table setting. The flowers and fruit can be dried to provide decorations and gifts. The evocative scents of roses can be preserved in cosmetic rose oil (your own preparation) and in potpourris. You can even cook with roses to create delicate flavors or rose hip jams rich in vitamin C.

CUT ROSES

The best time to cut roses from your garden is in late afternoon, at dusk. The next-best time is in the early morning while the air is still cool. Roses cut during the heat of the day will quickly wilt for lack of moisture.

Choose flowers that are just opening or that have opened halfway. Because flowers with few petals unfold more quickly than those with many petals, single blooms will last longest if picked when they are barely starting to bloom. A sampling of various early stages of blooming will give your arrangement a less uniform, and therefore more interesting, appearance. It's better to leave flowers in full bloom on the plant; they're already near the end of their blooming cycle and will not last long when cut.

A rose, both plant and blossom, needs a continual supply of moisture to look its best and survive. Whenever it is deprived of moisture, it will start to wilt. Thus, it's a good idea to carry a bucket of tepid water with you when you cut your roses so that you can immediately plunge them, foliage and blossoms, into it.

Be somewhat sparing in the amount of foliage you cut with blossoms during a newly planted rose's first 2 or 3 years of life, so as to leave the plant with plenty of leaves to support its growth. After the plant has become established, you can cut stems as long as you want them, though you should leave at least two leaves above the main stem.

Use sharp shears or a knife to make a cut at a 45-degree angle, just above a five-leaflet leaf. New growth will originate from the base of this leaf.

Keep the flowers in a cool place out of drafts until you are ready to prepare and arrange them. You can slow the opening of buds further by keeping them in water in the refrigerator.

PREPARING AND CARING FOR ROSES IN ARRANGEMENTS

Your impulse may be simply to arrange the flowers in water and enjoy them, but if you follow the procedures given below your roses will look fresher and last days longer. These methods can also be used with roses from a florist.

Left: Bouquet of Old Garden Roses includes 'Sombreuil', 'Madame Hardy', Königin von Dänemark, and 'La Reine Victoria'. Above: Miniature blooms include 'Cinderella', 'Mary Marshall', 'Starina', and 'Over the Rainbow'.

Clockwise from front left, 'Little Darling', 'Redgold', 'Yankee Doodle', 'Sunsilk', and 'Redgold'.

Remove thorns and foliage that will be below the water level in your vase. Otherwise they will rot, producing bacteria that will shorten the life of the flowers.

They easy way to remove foliage is to take several layers of paper towel or cloth and use it to grasp the stem, at the same time pulling downward to the end of the stem. Larger thorns will easily break off if you gently push them from the side with your thumb. Never scrape the stem with a knife. The injuries to the stem will shorten the life of the flowers.

Give the rose a fresh cut at least ½ inch above the end of the stem. Cut at a sharp angle to expose as much cut surface to the water as possible.

After you recut each stem, immerse it in deep water that is too hot for your hand (about 120°F). Leave the roses in this warm bath until the water cools; then place the entire container in the refrigerator or a cool place for a couple of hours to condition the blooms. (Wilted roses can usually be revived by giving them a fresh cut and subjecting them to this hot tub-icebox treatment.)

When you are ready to arrange the roses, fill a vase with fresh water. Some gardeners add a floral preservative to the water; others consider sterile water the best medium; still others swear by a dash of a light soft drink, such as 7-Up or Sprite, in the water. Experiment and see what works best for you. If you do use a floral preservative, follow the directions carefully; too much will shock the roses beyond restoration.

To secure the roses in the vase, you can use a 2-inch wire netting balled into the bottom of the vase, a metal holder, pebbles, or florist's foam.

If you use florist's foam, soak it thoroughly in the water before you insert the flowers. Do not move the stem after you place it in the foam, because air pockets will form at the base of the stem, cutting off the water supply.

As you arrange the flowers, give each one a fresh slanted cut before you place it. Keep the finished bouquet in as cool a place as possible, away from heat vents or radiators and out of direct sunlight. Keep it out of drafts. Keeping the arrangement in a sheltered spot outside at night will also prolong its freshness. Add enough fresh water daily to keep the stems immersed up to two-thirds of their length. Better yet, change the water every day, adding new preservative if you wish. The flowers will last longer if you recut the bottom of the stems every day or so.

ARRANGING ROSES

The arrangement of flowers is a matter of personal taste. Some gardeners prefer a formal design in a high triangular shape. Others prefer an English-type mixed flower basket, a very simple arrangement with an Oriental flavor, or just a lone specimen rose in a bud vase.

Nowadays, the trend is definitely toward more natural bouquets, letting the flowers speak for themselves without contrivance. Don't go overboard; sometimes a little restraint produces a more striking composition, in which each flower can be appreciated individually and as part of the whole. The appearance of clusters of floribundas is often improved by thinning out the more fully opened flowers to allow the others to bloom unrestricted.

Choose containers that fit the mood of the room or the occasion. Select a vase that relates visually in size to the blooms. Gleaming silver or other metal reflects the beauty of roses. Tiny teacups, creamers, and other small-scale containers are perfect for miniatures. Wicker baskets are good choices for garden-fresh casual bouquets, while china, porcelain, or ceramic containers are best suited to more formal arrangements. Clear glass or crystal allows you to enjoy the entire rose including the stem. This look is most successful without the use of mechanical holders or florist's foam.

A single variety of rose can be used in one arrangement, or several varieties can be mixed together. Roses blend successfully with other garden flowers of complementary or contrasting colors. For greenery, rose foliage is always a sure bet, but you might try adding ferns or camellia, ivy, or any other kinds of leaves of shades and textures that are pleasing to you.

Mixed bouquet includes 'Duet', 'Honor', 'Bewitched', 'Charisma', 'Cathedral', 'Tropicana', and 'Angel Face'.

POTPOURRI

"The rose looks fair, but fairer it we deem for that sweet odor which doth in it live." When Shakespeare wrote these words, he may have been thinking of potpourri (pronounced poh-poo-REE). This traditional way to preserve the memories of the rose garden is as delightful today as it has been for centuries.

The French called the concoction "rotten pot," because the moist method of making potpourri actually lets the petals slowly rot in a jar. When the jar was opened, the rose fragrance was released, relieving the stale atmosphere of damp, stuffy houses.

Today potpourri is most often made by the dry method, but both methods produce a mixture that can sweeten the air with its heady aroma. We'll give both general and specific directions for creating your own dry or moist potpourri. It's easy and fun to experiment with different scents and blends to create your own unique fragrance.

CREATING POTPOURRI

Cut roses in the early morning after the dew is gone. The fresher the flower, the more essential oil remaining after the flower is dried. The more fragrant cultivars (see page 91) will, of course, yield the more fragrant petals, but the roses you pick can contribute color, rather than scent, to your mixture. Potpourris need not be composed exclusively of roses; pick other fragrant garden flowers (lavender, violets, freesia), leaves, and herbs at the same time to mix with the roses.

Gently pull the petals from the flowers. You might wish to include some small leaves or tiny buds for further texture. Select an area away from strong light, where warm air can circulate, and spread the petals, leaves, and buds on a drying rack, preferably a wooden one, since metal can discolor the petals. You can also place the plant materials flat on layers of paper towels. Stir or turn them daily.

The petals for moist potpourri should be dried for only a few days, just until they are limp, not crisp. Petals for dry mixtures should be completely dried, until they are like cereal flakes. In dry potpourri a few damp petals can spoil a whole batch. Total drying usually takes from 4 days to 2 weeks, depending on the moisture in the petals and in the air.

If you are in a hurry, spread the petals on a cookie sheet and place them in a warm oven (110°F). Leave the door open to allow moisture to escape. Stir gently or shake the sheet from time to time so the petals will dry evenly. Drying usually takes 1 to 2 hours. Petals dried quickly like this lose more of their color intensity than do petals dried using the slower methods. The petals are now ready to be turned into potpourri.

The petals are mixed with fixatives to absorb the fragrant oils and preserve the fragrance. Common fixatives include orrisroot, benzoin, or storax. A quarter pound of any one of these is enough for a 1-quart potpourri.

Dry potpourri. Mix the petals with the fixative and add whatever spices and other fragrant materials you wish. Mix the materials well and store the mixture in a tightly covered container for several weeks until the fragrances blend and mellow. Then place the mixture in serveral containers with removable lids. If you use clear glass, you have the extra pleasure of being able to see the colors of the contents. You can also sew the mixture inside little bags or pillows (sachets) to use inside drawers or closets to give them a sweet smell.

Dry potpourri, delicate fabrics, ribbons, and lace create nostalgic sachets to freshen closets and drawers.

SAN FRANCISCO POTPOURRI

4 cups dried rose petals and small buds

½ cup dried rose leaves

½ cup dried rose geranium leaves

4 ounces dried orrisroot, coarsely crushed

2 tablespoons dried citrus peel, finely chopped

1 tablespoon whole cloves, crushed

1 tablespoon whole allspice

1 teaspoon anise seed, crushed

1 tablespoon cardamom seed, crushed

1 whole nutmeg, crushed

2 bay leaves, finely broken

4 cinnamon sticks, broken into 1-inch pieces
Several drops *each* oils of jasmine, rose geranium, and tuberose

1. Place the rose petals and leaves, along with the geranium leaves, in a large opaque container with a tight-fitting lid.

2. Add the orrisroot, citrus peel, and spices and mix together gently with your hands.

3. Sprinkle the oils on top. Close the container tightly and shake vigorously. Shake twice weekly for about 6 weeks, by which time the mixture will be well aged. Transfer the mixture to small decorative boxes and jars.

Moist potpourri. Moist potpourris have a heavier fragrance and last longer than the dry mixtures. The slightly dried petals are salted down—like making pickles—with noniodized salt in a crock, mixed with spices, fragrant oils, and a bit of brandy or perfume. These materials are stirred together daily for about a month until the scents are well blended and mellowed. It is a good idea to keep a weight on top of the petals to draw out all the oils.

When the blend is mellow, pour it into a large container, and mix well once again. Place in small porcelain, silver, or opaque glass containers with removable lids that can be opened whenever you wish to fill the room with the aroma of a summer day.

Whenever moist potpourri seems dry and is losing its fragrance, pour a small amount of good-quality brandy over the top and mix it in to reactivate the fragrant oils.

MOIST POTPOURRI

4 cups partially dried rose petals

2 cups mixed, partially dried, fragrant garden flowers (such as jasmine, orange blossoms, lavender, or violets)

1 cup dried fragrant leaves (such as rose geranium, lemon verbena, chamomile, or rosemary)

3 bay leaves

¾ cup noniodized table salt

¼ cup allspice, crushed

¼ cup cloves, mashed

¼ cup brown sugar

1 tablespoon dried orrisroot, coarsely crushed

2 tablespoons brandy

1. Crush the bay leaves into the salt with a mortar and pestle and mix together with the allspice, cloves, and sugar.

2. Blend the flower petals and leaves with the orrisroot. Place some of the petal mixture in a large crock that can be covered, and sprinkle with the salt mixture. Continue alternating layers of petals and salt.

3. Add the brandy. Cap tightly.

4. Open every day and stir.

5. After a month pour the materials into a large bowl and mix thoroughly. Fill small containers.

The aromatic ingredients of both moist and dry potpourri are gathered from around the world.

Encyclopedia of Roses

THIS ILLUSTRATED LIST OF OVER
250 VARIETIES OF ROSES
WILL HELP YOU CHOOSE ONE
[OR PROBABLY SEVERAL] THAT ARE
EXACTLY SUITED TO YOUR
LIKING AND NEEDS.

There are literally hundreds of different roses from which you can choose if you buy from mail-order suppliers. Your local nurseries and garden centers will usually have a much more limited selection of hybrid teas, floribundas, and grandifloras and climbers, though they often specialize in plants that are particularly well suited to your climate and region.

The encyclopedia listings starting on page 62 contain short descriptions of over 250 rose species and cultivars, with mail-order sources for each plant. In addition, we have provided short lists of various roses for specific landscape uses; by color; or for specific attributes, such as fragrance, long-lasting flowers, or disease resistance. These short lists are intended as a helpful starting point for you to select roses for your garden; they are not definitive, based as they are half on opinion and half on the growing experiences of many gardeners throughout North America.

The encyclopedia is divided into eight sections according to the major classifications of roses: species roses, modern shrub roses, old garden roses, hybrid teas, floribundas and polyanthas, grandifloras, climbers, and miniatures. The first column gives the name of the rose (with any synonymous cultivar names in parentheses), the year of introduction, and any awards bestowed by the American Rose Society (ARS) and the All-America Rose Selection (AARS) judges.

The next column gives an imprecise description of the flower color—imprecise in that words are often ambiguous and inexact generalizations of a whole range of shades.

The third column gives further details on the flowers: size, single, semidouble, or double; fragrance; frequency and amount of bloom; and any other particular features.

The next column describes the appearance of the foliage; plant size and growth habit; and any cultural advantages or drawbacks, such as hardiness or susceptibility to mildew. Keep in mind that the mature size of a plant is a relative matter: The size of the plant will depend on many interrelated factors, including your climate and the length of the growing season in your area; the amount of water, fertilizer, and pest control the plant receives, as well as the degree of pruning you give it.

The last column lists numbers corresponding to the list of mail-order suppliers on page 92 from whom you can order the rose. The suppliers coded for each rose listed were determined at the time of publication. Please note, though, that the availability of specific roses may vary considerably from year to year. Always reconfirm the availability of specific roses with a current catalog.

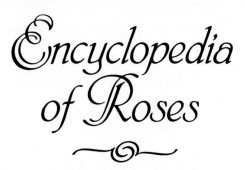

A modern rose and an old rose. Left: Rich pink-purple bloom of hybrid tea 'Miss All-American Beauty'. Above: The fragrant Rosa gallica officinalis 'Van Vlack'.

Rosa eglanteria

Top: Rosa × harisonii
Above: Rosa hugonis

Top: Rosa laevigata
Above: Rosa foetida bicolor

SPECIES ROSES

Rose, year of introduction, awards, and ARS rating*	Flower color	Flower description and blooming habits	Foliage, growth habits, and cultural tips	Catalog sources†
R. eglanteria (Rosa rubiginosa) (Sweet Brier Rose, Eglantine), 7.7	Pink	1 1/2"–2" single; slight scented bloom; foliage strongly smelling of pippin apples, especially when wet; làte May to early June bloom.	Small, scented; large, vigorous shrub to 14'; bright-red hips; hardy.	11, 12, 13, 37
Rosa banksiae (Lady Banks' Rose), 9.0	Yellow or white	1 1/2"–2" double; in prolific heavy clusters; variety 'Lutea' is yellow; variety 'Alba Plena' is white and scented; late spring to early summer.	Small, glossy; climber to 25'; resists aphids and diseases; hardy to −5°F.	11, 12, 13, 37
Rosa foetida bicolor (Austrian Copper), 8.0	Orange and coppery red with gold reverse	2"–3" single; strong orange-coppery red with a golden yellow center, in sprays along arching branches; questionable scent (like clean linseed oil).	Dark green; tall, arching to 7'–8'; very susceptible to blackspot, but flowers worth it.	10, 11, 12, 13, 33, 37, 38, 41
Rosa foetida persiana (Persian Yellow), 7.7	Chrome yellow	3" double; rich, strange scent; packed with petals; blooms midsummer.	Rich green; rounded shrub to 6'; smooth, brown stems with gray thorns; parent of today's yellow roses; hardy.	7, 14, 17, 25, 37
Rosa × harisonii (Harison's Yellow), 7.6	Bright yellow	2"–3" double; yeasty aroma; free flowering during May and June.	Gray green, delicate; tall, erect, 4'–6'; very hardy.	11, 12, 13, 22, 41

*American Rose Society Ratings (see page 27) 10.0—Perfect (not yet achieved); 9.9–9.0—Outstanding; 8.9–8.0—Excellent; 7.9–7.0—Good; 6.9–6.0—Fair; 5.9 and lower—Of questionable value. Roses without a number have not been rated.

†See page 89.

Top: Rosa rugosa
Above: Rosa moyesii

Top: Rosa rubrifolia
Above: Rosa virginiana

Rose, year of introduction, awards, and ARS rating	Flower color	Flower description and blooming habits	Foliage, growth habits, and cultural tips	Catalog sources
Rosa hugonis (Father Hugo Rose), 9.1	Light yellow	2″ semidouble; sweet fragrance; clustered on arching branches during May and June.	Small, gray-green leaves; large, 8′ x 8′; very hardy.	12, 13, 18
Rosa laevigata (Cherokee Rose), 7.0	White	3″–4″ single; gold stamens; scent of gardenias; borne in clusters in mid- to late June.	Glossy; trailer, climber, 15′–50′; naturalized in South.	11, 45
Rosa moyesii	Blood red	2 1/2″–3″ single; creamy stamens; slight scent; annual bloom in mid-June.	Delicate, lacy; large, awkward habit to 12′ x 10′; hardy once established.	13, 37
Rosa rubrifolia, 8.8	Pink	1 1/2″ single; light-yellow stamens; white, starlike center; June bloom; bright-red hips.	Soft, gray green with distinct purple sheen; arching to 5′; hardy.	12, 13, 14, 33, 37
Rosa rugosa (Japanese Rose, Ramanas Rose, Rugosa Rose), 7.5	Carmine	3 1/2″–4″ semidouble; cinnamon fragrance; repeat bloom, even while setting hips.	Rich green, deeply textured; upright, 3′–6′; hardy, disease resistant; suckering; hips large, round, and red orange; good for hedges.	6, 10, 11, 12, 13, 14, 18, 37, 41
Rosa virginiana	Pink	2″ single; sweet fragrance; a great mass of blooms in late June.	Glossy; dense shrub to 6′; colorful in fall; fairly hardy.	11, 13
Rosa wichuraiana (Memorial Rose), 7.8	White	1 1/2″ –2″; slightly fragrant; borne in clusters during July.	Glossy, bright green; trailing canes to 15′.	12, 48

'Constance Spry'

Top: 'Blanc Double de Coubert'
Above: 'Complicata'

'Frühlingsgold'

SHRUB ROSES

Rose, year of introduction, awards, and ARS rating	Flower color	Flower description and blooming habits	Foliage, growth habits, and cultural tips	Catalog sources
'Blanc Double de Coubert' (1892), 8.5	White	2″–3″ semidouble; very fragrant; papery, cupped petals.	Glossy, corrugated; 4′ x 5′; disease resistant; hardy.	11, 12, 13, 14, 37
'Buff Beauty' (1939), 7.3	Apricot yellow	3″ double; strong tea scent; profuse blossoms, recurrent.	Dark, glossy; vigorous, arching to 6′; good for banks, fences; healthy.	11, 13, 22, 33, 37
'Cerise Bouquet' (1958), 8.1	Dark red	Medium size, semidouble; raspberry fragrance; blooms in midsummer.	Grayish, small; large, open bush, 6′ x 6′.	11, 33
'Complicata' (unknown)	Pink with white center	5″ single; yellow stamens; blooms along length of branch.	Large, light green; vigorous shrub or pillar to 5′ x 8′; spectacular in full flower.	11, 14
'Constance Spry' (1961)	Pink	3 1/2″–5″ double; strong scent; midsummer bloom.	Dark; large, vigorous, 7′ x 7′, arching; good for hedge or on fence or pillar.	11, 33, 37
'Frau Dagmar Hastrup' ('Frau Dagmar Hartopp'), (1914) 8.9	Silvery pink	3″ single; golden-yellow stamens; strong fragrance; continuous bloom in clusters.	Dark, textured; compact growth to 2 1/2′–3′; good low hedge; hardy; large crimson hips; rugosa hybrid.	11, 12, 13, 37
'Frühlingsgold' (1937) ('Spring Gold')	Golden yellow	3 1/2″–5″ single; yellow stamens; strong fragrance; a magnificent display in spring, sometimes a second bloom in the fall.	Gray green; strong, dense growth to 7′ x 7′.	37

'Sparrieshoop'

Top: 'Stanwell Perpetual'
Above: 'Schneezwerg'

Top: 'Golden Wings'
Above: 'Pink Grootendorst'

Rose, year of introduction, awards, and ARS rating	Flower color	Flower description and blooming habits	Foliage, growth habits, and cultural tips	Catalog sources
'Golden Wings' (1956) ARS Gold Medal Certificate 1958, 8.5	Sulfur yellow	4 1/2" semidouble; lightly scented; repeat bloom.	Deep yellowish green; free branching, compact 4' x 4'; hardy.	12, 13, 22, 33
'Nevada' (1927), 8.2	White	4"–5" semidouble; not scented; sometimes pink tints; hundreds of blooms almost hiding foliage; recurrent.	Soft green, small; vigorous, arching, rounded shrub to 7'.	12, 13, 14
'Pink Grootendorst' (1923), 8.9	Clear pink	Small double; no scent; carnationlike; good cut; recurrent.	Small, wrinkled; bushy, prickly, to 4'; hardy; rugosa hybrid.	7, 10, 12, 13, 14, 17, 22, 33
'Schneezwerg' (1912) ('Snowdwarf'), 7.3	Pure white	3"–3 1/2" semidouble, like a Japanese anemone; fragrant; always in bloom even while setting hips.	Deep apple green, textured; bushy to 5'; healthy, hardy; good hips; rugosa hybrid.	12, 13, 33, 48
'Sparrieshoop' (1953), 7.9	Apricot pink	4" single to semidouble, very fragrant; abundant bloom in clusters or singly.	Leathery foliage; red thorns; upright, vigorous plant.	13, 19, 37
'Stanwell Perpetual' (1838), 8.0	Pink fading to white	3 1/2" double; strong fragrance; buff-yellow stamens; creased petals; summerlong blooming.	Neat, grayish green; thorny stems arching to 6', often rather loose, straggling growth if not supported.	11, 13, 33

Rosa tuscany

Top: *Rosa gallica versicolor*
Above: 'Madame Hardy'

Top: *Rosa gallica officinalis*
Above: *Rosa damascena semperflorens*

OLD GARDEN ROSES

Rose, year of introduction, awards, and ARS rating	Flower color	Flower description and blooming habits	Foliage, growth habits, and cultural tips	Catalog sources
GALLICA				
Rosa gallica officinalis (before 1300) (Apothecary Rose, Double French Rose, Red Rose of Lancaster), 9.3	Red	2"–3" semidouble; strong fragrance; used in potpourri and attar of roses; midsummer bloom.	Rough, dark; medium size, to 4'; suckers; hardy.	11, 13, 33, 37
Rosa gallica versicolor (possibly before 1581) (Rosa Mundi), 9.1	Striped red, pink, and white	2"–3" semidouble; light fragrance; flaring petals.	Rough, dark; low, sprawling to 3'; sport of *Rosa gallica*.	11, 33, 37
'Tuscany Superb' (before 1848), 8.0	Dark crimson purple	4"–5" semidouble; yellow stamens; slight fragrance; velvety petals.	Rough, dark; vigorous bush 2'–3'; hardy.	11, 33, 37
DAMASK				
'Madame Hardy' (1832), 8.8	White	2 1/2"–3 1/2" double; strong fragrance; distinctive emerald-green button eye.	Clear green; thickly foliaged bush to 6'; hardy.	12, 13, 37
Rosa damascena semperflorens (Rosa damascena bifera) (ancient) (Autumn Damask), (Rose des Quatre Saisons)	Pink	3 1/2" double; *very* fragrant, useful for potpourri and rose oil; crumpled petals; recurrent in warm climates.	Rough, light green; vigorous bush to 5'; hardy.	33, 37
Rosa damascena versicolor (before 1700) (York and Lancaster Rose), 8.1	White and pale pink	1 1/2"–2 1/2" semidouble; moderate fragrance; sometimes pink, sometimes white, or having differently colored petals, not striped.	Rounded, full green; vigorous bush to 5'.	12, 13, 33, 37

Top: 'Fantin-Latour'
Above: Rosa centifolia cristata

Rosa damascena versicolor

'Königin von Dänemark'

Rose, year of introduction, awards, and ARS rating	Flower color	Flower description and blooming habits	Foliage, growth habits, and cultural tips	Catalog sources
ALBA				
'Célestial' (late 1700s) ('Celeste'), 7.5	Soft pink	3 1/2" semidouble; sweet fragrance; half-opened buds, borne in clusters, of particular beauty.	Blue green; vigorous shrub to 6'; known for its unique complement of foliage and flower.	11, 12, 33
'Great Maiden's Blush' (before 1738) (Now classified as *Rosa alba incarnata*)	Blush pink	2"–3" double; moderate fragrance; early summer bloom.	Gray green; vigorous to 5'; hardy.	11, 13, 33, 37
'Königin von Dänemark' (1826) ('Queen of Denmark'), 8.1	Flesh pink	2 1/2"–4" double; strong fragrance; dark-pink buds; button eye.	Blue green; loose, spreading to 7'; hardy.	11, 13, 33, 37
CENTIFOLIA				
'Fantin-Latour' (unknown), 7.6	Soft pink	2"–3" double; delicate fragrance; flat; prolific summer bloom.	Dark, smooth; arching shrub to 5', benefits from support; hardy.	12, 33, 37
Rosa centifolia bullata (before 1815), 7.5	Pink	Large double; strong fragrance; globular.	Large, puckered, bronze when young; loose-growing shrub to 4'; hardy.	12, 13, 33
Rosa centifolia cristata ('Chapeau de Napoléon', Crested Moss), 8.7	Pink	2"–3" double; moderate fragrance; heavy frill of moss on sepals, though not a true moss rose; opening buds of special beauty.	Medium green, delicate; rounded, arching shrub to 4'; hardy.	13, 33, 37
Rosa centifolia pomponia (1789) (Rose de Meaux, Pompon Rose), 8.3	Pink	1"–1 1/2" double; strong fragrance; flat pom-pom.	Light green; small, to 3', with arching stems; dense, requiring pruning of twiggy growth.	11, 13, 33, 37

'Hermosa'

Top: 'Souvenir de la
Malmaison'
Above: 'Communis'

Top: 'La Reine Victoria'
Above: 'Old Blush'

OLD GARDEN ROSES

Rose, year of introduction, awards, and ARS rating	Flower color	Flower description and blooming habits	Foliage, growth habits, and cultural tips	Catalog sources
MOSS				
'Communis' (late 1600s) (Common Moss, Old Pink Moss, Pink Moss),8.7	Rose pink	2"–3" double; strong fragrance; reddish, mossed buds pine scented.	Dull green; rounded, arching shrub to 4'; hardy.	11, 12, 13, 33, 37
'Salet' (1854), 8.0	Rosy pink	2"–3 1/2" double; strong musk fragrance; opening flat; recurrent.	Light green; sturdy bush 3'–6'; hardy.	12, 13, 22, 33, 37
CHINA				
'Hermosa' (1840), 7.5	Light blush pink	1"–3" double; moderate fragrance; recurrent.	Gray green; small, to 3'; tender.	11, 13, 33
'Old Blush' (1752) ('Parson's Pink China', Old Pink Daily, Old Pink Monthly, Common Monthly), 7.9	Two-tone pink	1 1/2"–2 1/2" semidouble; moderate fragrance; borne in clusters; recurrent.	Soft green; medium bush to 5'; tender.	11, 33, 37
BOURBON				
'Honorine de Brabant' (1800s), 7.7	Pale lilac pink spotted and streaked with mauve and crimson	3 1/2"–4" double; raspberry fragrance; streaked and spotted petals; often a second bloom.	Light green, smooth; rampant grower to 5'; tender.	11, 33, 37
'La Reine Victoria' (1872), 8.1	Rich pink	1 1/2"–2 1/2" double; delicate fragrance; repeat bloom.	Narrow, smooth; erect to 6'; tender; appreciates support.	12, 13, 33, 37
'Souvenir de la Malmaison' (1843) ('Queen of Beauty and Fragrance'), 8.5	Creamy flesh with rosy center	1 1/2"–4" double; spicy fragrance; fading to almost white; recurrent.	Medium green; shrub or pillar rose; vigorous to 6'; tender.	11, 22, 33

'Comte de Chambord'

'Duchesse de Brabant'

Top: 'Baronne Prévost'
Above: 'Ferdinand Pichard'

Rose, year of introduction, awards, and ARS rating	Flower color	Flower description and blooming habits	Foliage, growth habits, and cultural tips	Catalog sources
PORTLAND				
'Comte de Chambord' (1860), 7.1	Pink-tinted lilac	3″–4 1/2″ double; fragrant; recurrent.	Deep green, pointed; vigorous to 4′; hardy.	11, 37
TEA				
'Duchesse de Brabant' (1857) ('Comtesse de Labarthe', 'Comtesse Ouwaroff'), 7.7	Soft rosy pink to bright rose	2″–3″ double; rich fragrance; upright, tuliplike buds; free blooming.	Glossy; upright bush to 4′; quite tender.	11, 22, 27
'Maman Cochet' (1893), 7.0	Pale pink with lemon yellow base	3″–4″ double; moderate fragrance; single flowering in June.	Dark green, glossy; medium-size bush, to 4′; quite tender.	11, 37
NOISETTE				
'Lamarque' (1830)	White with yellow center	2″ double; light fragrance; recurrent.	Light green; vigorous climber to 15′; tender.	11, 22
HYBRID PERPETUAL				
'Baronne Prévost' (1842), 7.0	Rose pink, shading lighter	3″–4″ double; moderate fragrance, borne in clusters; good repeat bloom.	Medium green; tall, vigorous to 5′; fairly hardy.	11, 12, 37
'Ferdinand Pichard' (1921), 7.9	Striped pink and scarlet	2 1/2″–4″ double; little scent; spring and fall blooms.	Yellowish green; medium tall, to 5′; responds to pegging if low spreader is desired.	12, 13, 33, 37
'Général Jacqueminot' (1853) ('General Jack', Jack Rose), 6.8	Red	2 1/2″–4″ double; very fragrant; strong stems; spring and fall blooms; velvety petals.	Rich green; vigorous to 6′.	13, 33, 37

'Candy Stripe'

Top: 'American Heritage'
Above: 'Bing Crosby'

Top: 'Brandy'
Above: 'Bewitched'

HYBRID TEA ROSES

Rose, year of introduction, awards, and ARS rating	Flower color	Flower description and blooming habits	Foliage, growth habits, and cultural tips	Catalog sources
'American Heritage' (1965) AARS 1966, 7.5	Ivory edges tinged with salmon	3"–5" double; no fragrance; moderate blooming.	Dark, leathery; tall, to 5'.	31, 33, 38
'Antigua' (1974), 7.2	Apricot blend	4 1/2"–6" double; fruity, spicy fragrance; lasts well.	Glossy, bronze, leathery; tall, upright bush; disease resistant.	2, 16, 41
'Arkansas' (1980)	Paprika red	Large double; fragrant; abundant blooms borne singly on long, sturdy stems.	Leathery, dark green; tall, vigorous, upright; disease resistant.	4, 41, 43, 45
'Autumn Gold' (1969), 6.5	Butterscotch and yellow blend	Medium double; fragrant; darker shades in center; strong stems.	Dark green, glossy; medium height; well branched; disease resistant.	4, 43, 45
'Bewitched' (1967) AARS 1967, 7.4	Pure pink	5" double; spicy, old-fashioned fragrance; long, pointed buds.	Glossy; tall, bushy; disease resistant; easy to grow.	1, 2, 5, 33, 38, 40, 41, 43, 45
'Big Ben' (1964), 7.5	Dark red	5"–6" double; heavy fragrance; sparse bloomer.	Dark green; tall bush.	10, 38, 44
'Bing Crosby' (1980) AARS 1981, 7.5	Persimmon orange to red	3 1/2"–4" double; moderate fragrance; long stems.	Glossy, bright green; vigorous, bushy, medium height; disease resistant.	1, 2, 3, 4, 5, 6, 8, 15, 16, 17, 29, 38, 41, 43, 45, 48
'Blue Moon' (1964) ('Mainzer Fastnacht'), 7.4	Lilac	4" double; heavy fragrance; free blooming; good cut.	Dark green, leathery; vigorous; fairly hardy; disease resistant.	5, 31, 33
'Brandy' (1982) AARS 1982	Golden apricot	Large double; tea fragrance.	Large, semiglossy; strong, bushy plant; disease resistant.	1, 2, 3, 4, 5, 6, 15, 25, 29, 38, 40, 41, 43, 44, 45, 48
'Candy Stripe' (1963), 6.5	Dusty pink with lighter stripes	6" double; heavy fragrance; free blooming.	Dark green, leathery; well-shaped bush to 4'.	41, 43
'Charlotte Armstrong' (1940) AARS 1941, 7.5	Cerise becoming red	3"–4" double; light tea fragrance; free blooming on long stems; excellent cut.	Dark, leathery; very vigorous, medium-size bush; easy to grow.	1, 2, 4, 7, 15, 29, 31, 38, 41, 43, 45

'Dainty Bess'

'Color Magic'

Top: 'Chrysler Imperial'
Above: 'Chicago Peace'

Rose, year of introduction, awards, and ARS rating	Flower color	Flower description and blooming habits	Foliage, growth habits, and cultural tips	Catalog sources
'Chicago Peace' (1962), 8.3	Pink with canary yellow base	5"–5 1/2" double; slight fragrance; more intense color than 'Peace'; good cut.	Glossy, leathery; vigorous, upright, bushy; medium height.	1, 2, 4, 5, 10, 13, 14, 15, 17, 18, 29, 31, 33, 38, 40, 41, 43, 44, 45, 48
'Christian Dior' (1958) AARS 1962, 7.6	Crimson flushed scarlet	4"–4 1/2" double; slight fragrance; abundant blooms; good cut.	Dark, glossy, leathery; tall, bushy plant; susceptible to mildew.	38, 41, 43, 44, 45
'Chrysler Imperial' (1952) AARS 1953, ARS Gold Medal Certificate 1956, James Alexander Gamble Rose Fragrance Medal 1965, 8.1	Crimson red with darker shading	4 1/2"–5" double; heavy, spicy fragrance; moderate blooming; long stems; good cut.	Dark green; upright bush to 4'; needs summer heat to perform well.	1, 2, 4, 5, 6, 7, 10, 13, 14, 15, 17, 18, 25, 29, 33, 38, 40, 41, 43, 44, 45, 48
'Color Magic' (1978) AARS 1978, 8.0	Ivory to deep rose	6"–7" double; color darkening with age; slight fragrance.	Large, dark green, glossy; vigorous; medium height; disease resistant; needs extra winter protection in colder climates.	2, 4, 5, 6, 15, 16, 29, 31, 38, 41, 43, 44, 45
'Command Performance' (1970) AARS 1971, 7.2	Orange red	3"–4" semidouble; heavy fragrance; free blooming, spring to frost.	Leathery, coarse; upright growth to 4 1/2'; performs poorly in humid weather; susceptible to mildew.	4, 14, 15, 33, 38
'Confidence' (1951), 8.0	Light pink to yellow blend	3"–5" double; intense fragrance; profuse bloom.	Dark, leathery; vigorous grower to 4'.	5, 31, 33, 44, 45
'Crimson Glory' (1935) James Alexander Gamble Rose Fragrance Medal 1961, 7.4	Deep crimson with purple shadings	3"–4" double; heavy old-fashioned fragrance; good cut.	Dark green, glossy; vigorous and spreading to 4'; best in warm climates.	1, 2, 4, 7, 11, 15, 29, 31, 37, 38, 40, 41, 43, 45
'Dainty Bess' (1925), 8.8	Rose pink	3"–4" single; golden orange stamens; moderate fragrance; ruffled edges on petals.	Abundant, leathery; vigorous, upright bush to 4'; hardy.	4, 5, 6, 13, 37, 41, 43, 45, 48

'Duet'

Top: 'Fragrant Cloud'
Above: 'First Love'

Top: 'Electron'
Above: 'Double Delight'

HYBRID TEA ROSES

Rose, year of introduction, awards, and ARS rating	Flower color	Flower description and blooming habits	Foliage, growth habits, and cultural tips	Catalog sources
'Double Delight' (1977) AARS 1977, 8.8	Creamy white becoming red	5 1/2″–6″ double; heavy, spicy fragrance; prolific; excellent cut; amount of red dependent on heat, increasing with age.	Dark, glossy; spreading, quite bushy; medium height; somewhat tender; disease resistant.	1, 2, 3, 4, 5, 6, 8, 15, 16, 17, 25, 29, 31, 38, 40, 41, 43, 44, 45,48
'Duet' (1960) AARS 1961, 8.0	Light and dark pink	2″–4″ double in clusters; slight scent; prolific; petals light pink inside, darker outside; good color retention; excellent cut.	Glossy, hollylike; vigorous, bushy to 4′ and higher; disease resistant; excellent for hedges.	1, 5, 14, 31, 38, 43
'Electron' (1970) AARS 1973, 8.1	Rose pink	3″–5″ double; fragrant; very free blooming; good retention of intense color.	Lush, dark green; vigorous and bushy to 3′; disease resistant.	5, 14, 31, 33, 38, 41, 43
'First Love' (1951), 7.5	Rose to pink	2 1/2″–3 1/2″ double; slight fragrance; long, slender buds; free blooming.	Graceful, long, light green; tall, slender bush.	5, 31, 37, 38, 43
'First Prize' (1970) AARS 1970, 9.1	Rose pink with ivory center	6″ double; moderate fragrance; abundant blooms; long stems; excellent cut.	Dark, leathery, abundant; medium height, spreading; resistant to blackspot; tender in cold climates.	1, 2, 4, 5, 15, 16, 17, 31, 33, 38, 41, 42, 43, 44, 45
'Fragrant Cloud' (1963) ('Duftwolke') James Alexander Gamble Rose Fragrance Medal 1969, 8.1	Coral red becoming geranium red	5″ double; color darkening with age; heavy tea fragrance; free blooming; good cut.	Dark, glossy; vigorous, upright, to medium height; easy to grow.	1, 4, 5, 14, 16, 17, 31, 33, 38, 41, 43, 45
'Friendship' (1978) AARS 1979, 7.5	Deep pink	5 1/2″–6″ double; sweet fragrance; long, straight stems; good cut; good color retention.	Abundant, large, dark; tall bush; disease resistant; hardy.	2, 4, 5, 29, 31, 41, 43, 44, 48
'Futura' (1975), 7.5	Vermilion	4″–5″ double; moderate fragrance; profuse bloom; good color retention; good cut.	Deep green; vigorous, well branched; disease resistant; easy to grow.	2, 31, 43
'Garden Party' (1959) AARS 1960, 8.7	Pale yellow fading to white and light pink at edges	4″–5″ double; slight fragrance; free blooming.	Dark green, semiglossy, abundant; vigorous, bushy, medium height; disease resistant except sometimes mildew; very winter hardy.	1, 2, 4, 5, 7, 13, 14, 15, 17, 18, 31, 33, 38, 40, 42, 43, 44, 45, 48

'Irish Gold'

Top: 'Honor'
Above: 'Lady X'

'Granada'

Rose, year of introduction, awards, and ARS rating	Flower color	Flower description and blooming habits	Foliage, growth habits, and cultural tips	Catalog sources
'Granada' (1963) AARS 1964, James Alexander Gamble Rose Fragrance Medal 1968, 8.7	Rose, red, and yellow blend	4″–5″ double; rich fragrance; long lasting; free blooming.	Hollylike; vigorous, upright, medium height; resistant to blackspot.	1, 2, 4, 5, 14, 31, 33, 38, 41, 43
'Helen Traubel' (1951) AARS 1952, 7.0	Pink to apricot	5″–6″ double; fruity fragrance; profuse blooms but with weak stems.	Leathery, olive green; vigorous and bushy to 3′. Good for hedge.	1, 4, 6, 7, 15, 18, 29, 31, 38, 41, 43
'Honor' (1980) AARS 1980, 8.0	Pure white	5″ double; light fragrance; long buds; prolific blooms.	Olive green; vigorous, upright, tall; good disease resistance.	1, 2, 3, 4, 5, 6, 8, 14, 15, 16, 17, 25, 38, 41, 43, 45, 48
'Irish Gold' (1966) ('Grandpa Dickson'), 7.0	Yellow	7″ double; moderate fragrance; long-lasting blooms, tinged with pink in cool weather.	Leathery, olive green; short, upright plant; likes frequent fertilizing.	2, 5, 38, 43
'King's Ransom' (1961) AARS 1962, 7.2	Golden yellow	5″–6″ double; moderate fragrance; holds color well.	Glossy, leathery; vigorous, upright to 3′; not hardy.	1, 2, 4, 5, 6, 15, 16, 17, 25, 29, 31, 33, 38, 40, 41, 43, 44, 45
'Kordes' Perfecta' (1957), 7.1	Cream, crimson, and yellow	4″–5″ double; heavy tea fragrance; colors deepening in hot weather.	Dark, glossy; compact; fairly hardy; best in partial shade in hot-weather climate.	2, 4, 6, 7, 25, 33, 38, 44
'Lady X' (1966), 8.5	Mauve	Large double; slight fragrance; abundant bloom.	Large, dark green; tall, strong, upright plant; very hardy.	4, 5, 31, 33, 43, 45
'Medallion' AARS 1973, 7.0	Apricot buff	7″–8″ double; moderate, fruity fragrance; good cut; long lasting.	Leathery, light green; tall, spreading; few thorns; disease resistant; fairly hardy; good for hedges.	1, 2, 4, 5, 6, 15, 16, 31, 33, 38, 43, 44, 45
'Michèle Meilland' (1945), 7.9	Bright pink shaded lilac with salmon center	3″–4″ double; moderate fragrance; color deepening to apricot in cool weather; good cut.	Light green; vigorous, bushy to 3′.	5, 11, 31, 33, 37

'Paradise'

Top: 'National Trust'
Above: 'Mon Cheri'

Top: 'Olympiad'
Above: 'Oregold'

HYBRID TEA ROSES

Rose, year of introduction, awards, and ARS rating	Flower color	Flower description and blooming habits	Foliage, growth habits, and cultural tips	Catalog sources
'Miss All-American Beauty' (1965) ('Maria Callas') AARS 1968, 8.7	Dark pink	4″–5″ double; heavy tea fragrance; free blooming; good color retention; good cut.	Leathery; bushy, tall, to 4′; disease resistant.	1, 2, 4, 5, 14, 33, 38, 43, 44, 45, 48
'Mister Lincoln' (1964) AARS 1965, 8.7	Dark red	4 1/2″–6″ double; rich, deep fragrance; moderate-to-free blooming; very good cut.	Large, dark, leathery; sturdy, upright to over 4′; hardy; disease resistant; easy to grow.	1, 2, 3, 4, 5, 6, 7, 10, 14, 15, 17, 25, 29, 31, 33, 38, 40, 41, 42, 43, 44, 45, 48
'Mon Cheri' (1982) AARS 1982	Deep red with pink	5″ double; blooms profusely.	Vigorous, bushy, medium height.	1, 2, 3, 4, 5, 6, 8, 15, 16, 25, 29, 38, 40, 41, 43, 44, 45, 48
'National Trust' (1970), 7.0	Bright red	Large double; slight scent; free blooming; extremely good color retention.	Bronze green; vigorous, bushy to 3′; healthy.	5, 31, 43
'Neue Revue' (1962), 6.9	Cream edged with scarlet	Large double; slight scent; free blooming.	Medium green; medium height; thorny; prefers warm nights.	5, 31, 33
'Oklahoma' (1964), 6.8	Very dark red	4″–5 1/2″ double; heavy musk fragrance; good cut.	Dark, leathery; well-branched bush to 4′; needs extra cold-winter protection; susceptible to mildew.	1, 2, 4, 7, 8, 14, 29, 31, 33, 40, 41, 43, 45
'Olympiad' (1983) AARS 1984	Crimson	4″–5″ double; little fragrance; borne singly or in small clusters on long, strong stems; abundant bloom.	Medium green; bushy to 3′–5′; good disease resistance; fairly hardy.	1, 3, 5, 8, 10, 15, 16, 25, 29, 40, 42, 43, 45
'Oregold' (1975) AARS 1975, 7.5	Deep yellow	5″ double; slight fragrance; colorfast; continuous blooms; good cut.	Dark, glossy; vigorous, upright to 4′; disease resistant.	1, 2, 3, 4, 5, 6, 8, 15, 16, 25, 29, 31, 38, 41, 43, 44, 45, 48

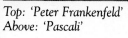

'Peace'

Top: 'Peter Frankenfeld'
Above: 'Pascali'

Top: 'Perfume Delight'
Above: 'Pristine'

Rose, year of introduction, awards, and ARS rating	Flower color	Flower description and blooming habits	Foliage, growth habits, and cultural tips	Catalog sources
'Papa Meilland' (1963) James Alexander Gamble Rose Fragrance Medal, 1974, 7.7	Dark crimson	Large double; heavy, old-fashioned fragrance; prolific blooms.	Glossy, leathery; olive green; vigorous, upright growth to 3'; blooms even in cold, wet springs.	5, 31, 33
'Paradise' (1978) AARS 1979, 8.0	Silvery lavender with ruby edging	5" semidouble; light fragrance; red spreading into lavender as flower unfolds; good cut.	Glossy, deep green; vigorous, very bushy to 3 1/2'; disease resistant.	1, 2, 4, 5, 6, 8, 15, 25, 29, 38, 40, 43, 44, 45
'Pascali' (1963) AARS 1969, 8.4	Cream	3"–4" double; slight fragrance; abundant flowers; good cut.	Dark, glossy; vigorous, bushy to 4'; very disease resistant.	1, 4, 5, 6, 14, 29, 31, 33, 38, 40, 42, 43, 44, 45, 48
'Peace' (1945) AARS 1946, ARS Gold Medal Certificate 1948 (the first winner of this award), 8.5	Yellow with pink edges	5"–6" double; slight fragrance; voted the world favorite rose; good cut.	Very dark, glossy; very vigorous, bushy, tall, to 4'; disease resistant; hardy.	1, 2, 3, 4, 5, 6, 7, 8, 10, 11, 13, 14, 15, 17, 18, 25, 29, 31, 33, 38, 40, 41, 42, 43, 44, 45, 48
'Perfume Delight' (1973) AARS 1974, 7.7	Deep pink	4 1/2"–5" double; heavy, spicy fragrance; abundant bloom; excellent cut.	Large, leathery, olive green; bushy, upright to 3'–4'; disease resistant.	1, 2, 3, 4, 6, 31, 33, 38, 40, 41, 43, 44, 45, 48
'Peter Frankenfeld' (1966), 7.8	Rose pink	6"–7" double; slight fragrance; good cut. Flowers smaller in warmer climates.	Deep green, closely set; upright to 3'; disease resistant; hardy.	5, 13, 31, 33
'Pink Favorite' (1956), 7.4	Deep pink, darker reverse	3"–4" double; slight scent; solid, abundant blooms on strong stems; good cut.	Distinctive, shiny, large, vigorous to 3'; hardy; disease resistant.	2, 5, 31, 33, 38
'Pristine' (1978), 8.0	Ivory with pink wash	5"–6" double; slight fragrance; prolific blooms; good cut.	Glossy, dark reddish green; medium height, spreading; very disease resistant; very hardy.	1, 2, 5, 16, 29, 31, 38, 41, 43, 45

'Swarthmore'

Top left: *'Seashell'*
Left: *'Sutter's Gold'*
Above: *'Red Devil'*

HYBRID TEA ROSES

Rose, year of introduction, awards, and ARS rating	Flower color	Flower description and blooming habits	Foliage, growth habits, and cultural tips	Catalog sources
'Proud Land' (1969), 7.2	Deep red	4 1/2″–5 1/2″ double; heavy tea fragrance; velvety petals; free blooming.	Abundant, dark, leathery; tall, vigorous, upright; disease resistant except for mildew; good for hedges.	2, 16, 31, 41
'Red Devil' (1970), 7.2	Light red with paler reverse	3 1/2″–4″ double; moderate fragrance; colorfast.	Glossy, medium green; tall, upright; good for coastal climates.	5, 31, 33, 38, 43
'Red Masterpiece' (1974), 7.2	Dark red	6″ double; heavy fragrance; excellent cut; good color retention.	Dark, leathery; vigorous bush, medium height; thick petals slow to open in foggy coastal areas; susceptible to mildew.	2, 16, 25, 31, 33, 41
'Rose Gaujard' (1957), 6.2	Cherry red with pink and silvery white reverse	3″–4″ double; slight fragrance; abundant blooms.	Glossy, dark green; vigorous, upright, spreading to 4′.	5, 31, 33, 38
'Royal Highness' (1962) AARS 1963, 8.5	Light pink	5″–5 1/2″ double; heavy tea fragrance; good form; abundant blooms; good cut.	Leathery, deep green; bushy, medium height 2 1/2′–4′; somewhat tender; resistant to mildew.	1, 4, 5, 15, 31, 33, 38, 41, 42, 43, 44, 45, 48
'Rubaiyat' (1946) AARS 1947, 7.3	Rose red, reverse lighter	4 1/2″–5″ double; heavy fragrance; free flowering.	Dense gray green, leathery; very vigorous, medium height; very hardy.	5, 31, 38
'Seashell' (1976) AARS 1976, 7.0	Burnt orange	3″–5″ double; color darkening with age; slight fragrance; abundant bloom.	Dark, hollylike; vigorous, bushy, of medium height; resistant to mildew and blackspot.	2, 3, 4, 5, 16, 38, 43, 44, 45
'South Seas' (1962), 7.5	Coral pink	6″–7″ double; moderate fragrance; ruffled petals; free blooming.	Large, leathery; vigorous, upright, medium height.	2, 41, 43, 44
'Spellbinder' (1975), 6.9	Ivory to crimson	6″ double; darkening with age; slight fragrance; mature plants prolific; long lasting; good cut.	Dark green, leathery; tall, upright bush; disease resistant.	2, 38

'Tiffany'

'Yankee Doodle'

Top right: 'Tropicana'
Right: 'White Masterpiece'

Rose, year of introduction, awards, and ARS rating	Flower color	Flower description and blooming habits	Foliage, growth habits, and cultural tips	Catalog sources
'Summer Sunshine' (1962), 7.3	Deep yellow	3 1/2"–5" double; slight fragrance; colorfast; free blooming.	Dusky, light green; vigorous, bushy, well branched, of medium height; somewhat tender.	1, 2, 5, 18, 31, 33, 38, 40, 41, 43
'Sutter's Gold' (1950) AARS 1950, James Alexander Gamble Rose Fragrance Medal 1966, 6.5	Golden orange tinged with salmon pink	4"–5" double; heavy, fruity fragrance; good cut.	Dark, glossy, leathery; very vigorous, spreading, 3'–4' tall; color retention best in cool weather; very disease resistant.	1, 2, 3, 4, 15, 29, 33, 38, 41, 43, 45
'Swarthmore' (1963), 8.6	Rose red	4" double; slight fragrance; many continuous blossoms; long lasting; good cut.	Dark, leathery; very vigorous, tall, to over 4'.	2, 5, 31, 33, 38
'Sweet Surrender' (1983) AARS 1983	Silvery pink	4 1/2"–5 1/2" double; generous archetypal rose fragrance; long, strong stems; free blooming.	Dark, leathery; vigorous, tall grower.	1, 2, 3, 5, 6, 7, 8, 15, 16, 25, 29, 38, 40, 43, 45
'Tiffany' (1954) AARS 1955, James Alexander Gamble Rose Fragrance Medal 1962, 8.8	Rose to pink	4"–5" double; exceptional fragrance; beautiful buds; free blooming; long lasting; good cut.	Dark; very vigorous, upright to over 4'; best performance in warm climates; disease resistant.	1, 2, 4, 5, 6, 7, 8, 14, 15, 17, 18, 25, 29, 31, 33, 38, 40, 41, 42, 43, 44, 45, 48
'Tropicana' (1960) ('Super Star') AARS 1963, ARS Gold Medal Certificate 1967, 8.4	Coral orange	4"–5" double; strong, fruity fragrance; colorfast; abundant blossoms; good cut.	Dark, glossy, leathery; vigorous to 4'–5'; spreading; easy to grow though somewhat prone to mildew.	1, 2, 3, 4, 5, 6, 7, 8, 10, 13, 14, 15, 16, 17, 18, 25, 29, 31, 33, 38, 40, 41, 42, 43, 44, 45, 48
'White Masterpiece' (1969), 7.6	White	6" double; light, sweet fragrance; exemplary form; continuous blooms; good cut.	Abundant, deep green, glossy; medium height, to 3', spreading; very disease resistant.	16, 31, 33, 38, 41, 43
'Yankee Doodle' (1965) AARS 1976, 7.2	Apricot to peach pink and butter yellow	5" double; slight tea fragrance.	Abundant, dark, glossy; vigorous, sturdy, bushy, tall; outstanding disease resistance.	1, 2, 4, 29, 43, 44, 45

'Angel Face'

'Cathedral'

Top: 'Cherish'
Above: 'Bahia'

FLORIBUNDA AND POLYANTHA ROSES Cultivars marked with an asterisk (*) are polyanthas.

Rose, year of introduction, awards, and ARS rating	Flower color	Flower description and blooming habits	Foliage, growth habits, and cultural tips	Catalog sources
'Angel Face' (1968), 8.0	Mauve lavender	4″ double; heavy, old-fashioned fragrance; good cut.	Dark, leathery; compact, bushy to 2′; disease resistant.	1, 2, 5, 6, 8, 14, 15, 16, 25, 29, 38, 41, 43, 44, 45, 48
'Bahia' (1974) AARS 1974, 7.0	Orange	2 1/2″–4″ double; light, spicy fragrance; free blooming.	Bronzy, glossy; upright, vigorous to 3′; disease resistant.	1, 4
'Betty Prior' (1935), 8.5	Carmine pink	2″–3″ single; moderate fragrance; very profuse and continuous blooms.	Glossy, dark; very vigorous to 4′–5′; hardy; disease resistant.	2, 4, 6, 13, 15, 38, 41, 44, 48
'Cathedral' (1975) AARS 1976, 7.4	Apricot to salmon	3″–3 1/2″ double; moderate fragrance; each small cluster a bouquet in itself; good cut.	Glossy, coppery green; upright, medium height; mildew resistant.	2, 4, 5, 14, 43
*'Cécile Brunner' (1881) (Sweetheart Rose, 'Mignon'), 7.6	Bright pink on yellow ground	1″–1 1/2″ double; moderate, sweet fragrance; exquisite buds; continuous bloom; good cut.	Tiny, dark, glossy; upright, 3′, few thorns.	11, 33, 38, 43, 45, 48
'Charisma' (1977) AARS 1978, 8.0	Scarlet and yellow	Small, double; slight fragrance; abundant and long lasting; good cut; red intensifying with age.	Leathery, glossy; compact, well branched, medium height.	2, 4, 5, 6, 8, 29, 38, 41, 43, 44, 45, 48
'Cherish' (1980), 8.0	Coral pink	3″–4″ double, almost hybrid tea size; light cinnamon fragrance; continual, abundant bloom over a long season; good cut.	Glossy, deep green; vigorous, spreading, medium height.	2, 4, 5, 6, 8, 15, 16, 17, 29, 31, 38, 41, 43, 44, 45, 48
*'China Doll' (1946), 8.0	Rose pink with yellow base	1″–2″ double; slight fragrance; continual masses of bloom covering plant.	Leathery; low growing, under 18″; good for borders, containers.	1, 4, 7, 38, 43, 44, 45, 48
'City of Belfast' (1968), 7.7	Bright red	3″ double; little scent; full, ruffled; continual abundant blooms.	Dark, glossy; medium height; resistant to rain damage and disease; tolerates partial shade; good for bedding.	5, 14
'Europeana' (1963) AARS 1968, 8.8	Dark crimson	3″ double; slight scent; many heavy clusters of long-lasting, nonfading blooms; good cut.	Red green; short, bushy; foliage and flowers down to the ground; disease resistant; easy to grow in all climates.	1, 5, 8, 14, 15, 25, 31, 33, 38, 41, 43, 44, 45, 48

'French Lace'

'Gene Boerner'

Top left: 'Eye Paint'
Top right: 'First Edition'
Above: 'Iceberg'

Rose, year of introduction, awards, and ARS rating	Flower color	Flower description and blooming habits	Foliage, growth habits, and cultural tips	Catalog sources
'Eye Paint' (1975), 8.0	Red blend	2 1/2″ single; showy golden stamens; slight scent; continuous bloom.	Small, dense, dark green; tall, spreading bush; susceptible to blackspot; best treated as a shrub, good for hedges.	5, 14, 31
'Fashion' (1949) AARS 1950, ARS Gold Medal Certificate 1954, 7.7	Coral peach	3″–3 1/2″ double; moderate fragrance; continual and abundant; nonfading.	Glossy, bronze; medium height, spreading; disease resistant.	2, 4, 13, 14, 15, 18, 25, 33, 38, 44, 48
'First Edition' (1976) AARS 1977, 8.4	Coral, shaded orange	2 1/2″ semidouble; slight fragrance; continual bloom; color deepening in cool climates; good cut.	Glossy, leathery, olive green; vigorous, medium height; good for containers.	2, 4, 41, 43, 45
'French Lace' (1981) AARS 1982	Ivory white with peach and pink tones	3″–4″ double; slight fragrance; 1–8 blossoms on single stem; continual bloom.	Dark green, hollylike; medium height, bushy; good disease resistance.	1, 2, 3, 4, 5, 6, 15, 16, 25, 38, 41, 43, 44, 45
'Garnette' (1951), 7.6	Garnet red with light yellow base	1″–2″ double; slight scent; long lasting.	Dark, leathery, ivylike; low growing, compact, vigorous.	7, 25, 37, 48
'Gene Boerner' (1968) AARS 1969, 8.7	Deep pink	2 1/2″–3 1/2″ double; slight tea fragrance; free blooming; perfect, smaller hybrid tea form.	Light green, glossy; medium-tall plant, upright; good disease resistance.	2, 4, 5, 33, 41, 43
'Ginger' (1962), 8.0	Orange scarlet	2 1/2″–3″ double; slight fragrance; long-lasting bloom; good cut.	Dark, glossy; small to medium; luxuriant foliage; somewhat hardy; disease resistant.	4, 5, 33
''Happy' (1954), 7.9	Garnet red	3/4″ semidouble; little fragrance; large clusters.	Deep green, fernlike; short, less than 2′; good for borders, containers.	5, 37
'Iceberg' (1958) ('Schneewittchen'), 8.9	Pure white	2″–4″ double; pleasant scent.	Glossy, light green; medium-to-tall rounded bush; vigorous, best if given space to grow; extremely hardy; disease resistant.	1, 5, 7, 13, 14, 15, 18, 31, 33, 37, 38, 40, 42, 43, 48
'Impatient' (1983) AARS 1984	Orange red	3″ double; slight fragrance; clusters on long stems; excellent repeat bloom.	New growth mahogany colored, turning dark green; 3′–4′ mound-shaped bush.	1, 3, 5, 8, 10, 15, 16, 25, 29, 40, 42, 43, 45

'Marina'

'The Fairy'

Top left: 'Redgold'   Above: 'Spartan'
Top right: 'Sun Flare'

FLORIBUNDA AND POLYANTHA ROSES Cultivars marked with an asterisk (*) are polyanthas.

Rose, year of introduction, awards, and ARS rating	Flower color	Flower description and blooming habits	Foliage, growth habits, and cultural tips	Catalog sources
'Intrigue' (1983) AARS 1984	Deep plum	3" double; rich, old-fashioned fragrance; small clusters; free blooming.	Glossy, dark green; medium height with upright growth; mildew resistant.	1, 3, 5, 8, 10, 15, 16, 25, 29, 40, 42, 43, 45
'Ivory Fashion' (1958) AARS 1959, 8.7	Ivory	4"–4 1/2" semidouble; moderate fragrance; free flowering; long lasting when cut.	Leathery; vigorous, upright to 2'–3'; disease resistant.	4, 31, 37, 43
***'Margo Koster'** (1931) ('Sunbeam'), 7.8	Salmon	1"–2" double; slight fragrance; free blooming.	Abundant, glossy; compact, to 24"; disease resistant; good for borders, containers.	2, 4, 13, 43, 44, 45, 48
'Marina' (1974) AARS 1981, 8.0	Orange with yellow base	2 1/2"–3" double; slightly fragrant; good cut.	Glossy, dark; bushy, compact, medium height; disease resistant.	2, 3, 4, 5, 6, 8, 15, 16, 25, 31, 38, 41, 43, 44, 45
'Orangeade' (1959), 8.0	Bright orange	2 1/2" semidouble; golden stamens; slight scent; abundant, long-lasting blooms; good cut.	Dark; medium-size bush; very sharp red thorns; hardy; disease resistant.	5, 31, 38
***'Perle d'Or'** (1884) ('Yellow Cécile Brunner'), 7.0	Amber yellow	1"–1 1/2" double; sweet scent; continual bloom.	Bright green, glossy; short bush, to 3'; very disease free.	11, 22, 37
'Redgold' (1971) ('Rouge et Or') AARS 1971, 7.9	Golden yellow edged deep pink	2"–3" double; slight scent; abundant and continual blooms; long lasting.	Glossy, light green; tall, vigorous bush to 2'–3'; disease resistant; allergic to some sprays.	2, 4, 5, 15, 16, 33, 41, 43
'Spartan' (1955) ARS Gold Medal Certificate 1961, 7.5	Orange red to reddish coral	3"–3 1/2" double; heavy fragrance; free blooming.	Dark, glossy; vigorous grower to 3'; disease resistant.	2, 4, 6, 14, 15, 29, 33, 42, 44, 45
'Sun Flare' (1983) AARS 1983	Lemon yellow	3" semidouble; mild licorice fragrance; free blooming.	Glossy, deep green; low, round, somewhat spreading bush; disease resistant.	1, 2, 3, 5, 6, 7, 8, 15, 16, 25, 29, 40, 43, 44, 45
***'The Fairy'** (1932), 8.6	Pink	1 1/2" double; slight fragrance; profuse blooms; large clusters of small flowers.	Glossy, dark, fernlike; short, 2 1/2', compact; very disease resistant; hardy.	2, 4, 5, 6, 8, 10, 13, 15, 18, 25, 33, 37, 38, 43, 45, 48

'Cherry-Vanilla'

'Love'

Top: 'John Armstrong'
Above: 'Camelot'

GRANDIFLORA ROSES

Rose, year of introduction, awards, and ARS rating	Flower color	Flower description and blooming habits	Foliage, growth habits, and cultural tips	Catalog sources
'Aquarius' (1971) AARS 1971, 7.7	Medium pink blend	4″ double; moderate fragrance; free blooming; long lasting when cut.	Leathery, large; medium-tall, upright bush; very disease resistant; hardy.	5, 31, 33, 38, 43
'Arizona' (1975) AARS 1975, 6.2	Golden bronze	4 1/2″ double; strong tea fragrance; colorfast; good cut.	Bronze green, semiglossy; tall bush, 4′–6′; disease resistant; excellent for mass plantings or tall hedge.	2, 4, 6, 38, 41, 43, 44, 45
'Buccaneer' (1952), 6.1	Bright yellow	3″–4″ double; slight tea fragrance; free blooming; nonfading; good cut.	Dark, leathery; very tall, upright, requiring lots of room; good for use as a tall hedge.	1, 4, 6
'Camelot' (1964) AARS 1965, 7.8	Salmon or shrimp pink	3 1/2″–4″ double; light, spicy fragrance; shades varying from orange to pink depending on weather; good cut.	Glossy, large; tall, upright, vigorous, needs room.	4, 14, 31, 33, 38, 43
'Cherry-Vanilla' (1973), 6.0	Creamy yellow to deep pink at edges	4 1/2″ double; moderate tea fragrance; profuse bloom.	Dark, leathery, semiglossy; upright, tall, bushy; disease resistant.	1, 38, 40
'Gold Medal' (1982)	Deep yellow	3 1/2″–4″ double; little fragrance; bud edged orange-red on deep gold; abundant blooms.	Large, glossy, deep green; tall, vigorous grower; remarkably winter hardy.	1, 5, 6, 40, 43, 45
'John S. Armstrong' (1961) AARS 1962, 7.3	Deep red	4″ double; slight fragrance; velvety petals; continuous bloom.	Deep green; medium height, bushy; disease resistant.	1, 14, 33
'Love' (1980) AARS 1980, 7.5	Scarlet with silvery white reverse	3 1/2″ double; spicy fragrance; free blooming; good cut.	Thick, medium green; broad, full bush; mildew resistant.	2, 3, 4, 5, 6, 8, 15, 16, 17, 29, 31, 41, 43, 44, 45, 48
'Mount Shasta' (1963), 7.7	White	4 1/2″–5″ double; moderate fragrance; free blooming; resembles a hybrid tea; good cut.	Leathery, gray green; tall, upright to 4′; good for cool-summer climates; somewhat tender; fairly disease resistant.	5, 14, 31, 33

'Shreveport'

'Prominent'

Top: 'Queen Elizabeth'
Above: 'Scarlet Knight'

GRANDIFLORA ROSES

Rose, year of introduction, awards, and ARS rating	Flower color	Flower description and blooming habits	Foliage, growth habits, and cultural tips	Catalog sources
'Olé' (1964), 8.2	Red orange	3 1/2" double; moderate scent; ruffled, camellialike, prolific, and long-lasting blooms; good cut.	Attractive, deep green, glossy; short, to 3'; bushy; disease resistant; tender.	1, 5, 38, 40, 41, 43
'Pink Parfait' (1960) AARS 1961, 8.9	Medium to light pink	3 1/2" double; slight fragrance; abundant blooms; good cut.	Bright green, glossy; vigorous, heavily branched, 2 1/2'–4'; disease resistant.	1, 5, 14, 31, 33
'Prominent' (1971) AARS 1977, 7.2	Hot orange	3" double; light, fruity fragrance; long-lasting, continuous bloom; colorfast.	Glossy, leathery; medium habit; disease resistant.	2, 5, 14, 16, 33, 38, 41
'Queen Elizabeth' (1954) AARS 1955, ARS Gold Metal Certificate 1960, 8.9	Carmine, rose, and pale pink	3 1/2"–4" double; moderate fragrance; profuse, continual, long-lasting blooms; excellent cut.	Dark, glossy; very vigorous and tall-growing to 4'–6'; very hardy; very disease resistant; a classic, deservedly so.	1, 4, 5, 6, 7, 13, 14, 15, 17, 18, 25, 29, 33, 38, 41, 42, 43, 44, 45, 48
'Scarlet Knight' (1966) ('Samourai') AARS 1968, 7.8	Scarlet	4"–5" double; slight fragrance; velvety petals; good color retention; free blooming; good cut.	Leathery; upright, bushy to over 4'; thorny; disease resistant.	25, 31, 33, 38, 43
'Shreveport' (1982) AARS 1982	Salmon and yellow blend	4" double; mildly fragrant.	Large, glossy; tall, bushy; hardy; disease resistant.	1, 2, 3, 4, 5, 6, 15, 25, 29, 38, 41, 43, 44, 45, 48
'Sonia' (1974), 8.2	Pink to coral to yellow	4" double; spicy fragrance; profuse, long-lasting bloom; good cut.	Deep green; bushy, medium height; disease resistant.	1, 5, 14, 15, 31, 33, 40, 41, 43, 48
'Sundowner' (1978) AARS 1979, 7.5	Golden orange	3 1/2"–4" double; heavily fragrant; profuse blooms.	Glossy, coppery dark green; tall plant; hardy; resistant to blackspot, prone to mildew.	2, 4, 5, 6, 8, 15, 29, 38, 41, 48
'White Lightnin' ' (1980) AARS 1981, 7.5	White	3" double; very fragrant; free blooming; good cut.	Dark, glossy; medium-height bush.	1, 2, 4, 6, 15, 31, 38, 40, 41, 43, 44, 45, 48

Top: 'America'
Above: 'Altissimo'

Top: 'Don Juan'
Above: 'Cecile Brunner'

CLIMBERS, RAMBLERS, AND PILLAR ROSES

Rose, year of introduction, awards, and ARS rating	Flower color	Flower description and blooming habits	Foliage, growth habits, and cultural tips	Catalog sources
'Altissimo' (1966) Large-flowered climber, 8.8	Scarlet	3 1/2"–4" single; long golden stamens contrasting with nonfading, velvety petals; little scent; almost continual blooming.	Dark green, serrated; to 15'; best if trained horizontally; excellent for posts, walls, fences, or arbors.	5, 43
'America' (1976) Large-flowered climber AARS 1976, 8.2	Coral pink	4"–5" double; spicy, carnationlike fragrance; hybrid tealike flowers; profuse bloomer all season.	Dark, leathery; moderately tall; disease resistant; hardy; easy to grow; good for pillars.	1, 2, 3, 4, 5, 6, 8, 15, 16, 25, 31, 38, 41, 43, 44, 45
'Climbing Baby Darling' (1972) Climbing miniature, 7.2	Apricot orange	1 3/4" double; slight fragrance; exquisite buds.	Medium green; grows to 3'–4'; excellent for containers; need extra support.	24, 26
'Blaze' (1932) Large-flowered climber, 7.9	Scarlet	2"–3" semidouble; slight fragrance; borne in large clusters; large spring bloom and smaller blooms throughout summer and fall.	Dark, leathery; fast growing to 12'–15'; hardy; disease resistant; widely planted, easy to grow.	1, 2, 3, 4, 6, 7, 8, 12, 13, 14, 15, 16, 17, 18, 25, 29, 31, 33, 38, 40, 41, 42, 43, 44, 45, 48
'Climbing Cécile Brunner' (1894) Climbing polyantha, 8.3	Bright pink on yellow ground	1"–1 1/2" double; moderate fragrance; strong blooms in spring and fall.	Dark; vigorous grower to 20'; good for trellises, arbors, or in open trees.	1, 2, 37, 38, 43, 48
'Climbing Crimson Glory' (1946) Climbing hybrid tea, 7.2	Deep crimson with purple shadings	3"–4" double; rich fragrance; good cut.	Leathery; vigorous grower to 10'; quite hardy; preferred by many gardeners to the bush variety.	2, 4, 29, 37, 45
'Don Juan' (1958) Large-flowered climber, 8.3	Dark red	4"–5" double; heavy fragrance; profuse, long-lasting flowers throughout season; good cut.	Dark, glossy, leathery; vigorous, upright grower to 8'; fairly hardy; disease resistant; excellent as a pillar rose.	1, 2, 3, 4, 5, 7, 8, 15, 18, 29, 31, 38, 41, 43, 44, 45

Top: 'Golden Showers'
Above: 'Joseph's Coat'

'Dortmund'

'Handel'

CLIMBERS, RAMBLERS, AND PILLAR ROSES

Rose, year of introduction, awards, and ARS rating	Flower color	Flower description and blooming habits	Foliage, growth habits, and cultural tips	Catalog sources
'Dortmund' (1955) Species (R. kordesii) hybrid, 9.0	Strawberry red with white center	2 1/2"–3 1/2" single; slight fragrance; large clusters throughout season.	Glossy, light green; vigorous, long, trailing canes to 10'; very disease resistant; hardy; tolerates some shade; can be allowed to form a large shrub or pegged as a ground cover.	5, 11, 12, 22, 33, 37
'Dr. W. Van Fleet' (1910) Large-flowered climber, 7.5	Blush pink fading to flesh white	2 1/2"–3" double; moderately fragrant; one profuse bloom in spring.	Glossy, dark; strong growth to 15'–20'; hardy; disease resistant.	11, 13, 22, 37
'Elegance' (1937) Large-flowered climber, 7.3	Medium yellow, edges fading to white	6" very double; fragrant; long, strong stems; somewhat recurrent.	Glossy; very vigorous growth to 10'–12'; good winter hardiness.	22, 33, 37
'Félicité et Perpétue' (1827) Species (R. sempervirens) sport	White blush to pale cream	1"–1 1/2" double; delicate primrose fragrance; large clusters; once blooming.	Semievergreen, glossy, blue green; vigorous growth to 12'–15'; disease resistant; fairly hardy.	12, 37
'Golden Showers' (1956) Large-flowered climber AARS 1957, 6.9	Daffodil yellow	4" double; moderate fragrance; long, almost thornless stems; profuse, continual bloom.	Dark, glossy; strong grower to 8'–12'; excellent pillar rose.	1, 2, 3, 4, 5, 6, 7, 8, 11, 13, 15, 17, 18, 25, 29, 33, 38, 40, 41, 42, 44, 45, 48
'Handel' (1965) Large-flowered climber, 7.8	Cream edged with rose red	3 1/2" double; pleasant, light scent; prolific bloomer throughout season.	Dark, glossy; vigorous grower to 12'–14'; will tolerate some shade; good for posts, walls, fences, small structures.	1, 5, 13, 31, 40, 43
'Joseph's Coat' (1964) Large-flowered climber, 7.5	Yellow and red	3" double; slight fragrance; very free blooming in a riot of bright colors all season long.	Dark, glossy; vigorous, small to medium height; somewhat tender; prone to mildew; can be planted as a shrub, pillar, or climber.	1, 2, 5, 8, 14, 15, 25, 29, 33, 38, 40, 43, 45, 48
'Kathleen' (1922) Hybrid musk, 7.0	Blush pink	1"–1 1/2" single; rich apple-blossom scent; very free blooming.	Glossy; 6'–15' semiclimber with training; orange hips; very disease resistant; quite hardy; can be used as a shrub, climbing, or pillar rose.	11, 12, 37

'Kathleen'

'Royal Sunset'

Top: 'Sombreuil'
Above: 'Mermaid'

Rose, year of introduction, awards, and ARS rating	Flower color	Flower description and blooming habits	Foliage, growth habits, and cultural tips	Catalog sources
'Mermaid' (1918) Species (R. bracteata) hybrid, 7.1	Pale sulfur yellow	5"–6" single; amber stamens; slight fragrance; free blooming.	Glossy, dark green, vigorous to over 20'; thorny; tender; resistant to blackspot.	11, 22
'New Dawn' (1930) Large-flowered climber, 8.0	Pink	2"–3" double; fragrant; profuse, continual bloom.	Glossy, dark; vigorous to 12'–20'; somewhat hardy; disease resistant.	4, 12, 13, 22, 33, 37, 41, 45
'Paul's Scarlet Climber' (1916) Large-flowered climber, 7.5	Scarlet shaded to crimson	2"–3" semidouble; slight scent; many large clusters; one flowering in spring.	Dark, leathery; vigorous growth to 10'–15'; very hardy.	4, 8, 10, 12, 15, 25
'Rhonda' (1968) Large-flowered climber, 7.5	Carmine rose	3"–4" double; slight fragrance; abundant, continuous bloom from spring; blooms first year; good cut.	Dark, glossy; restrained growth to 7'–8'; disease resistant; defies bad weather; easy to train; good in small spaces or as pillar rose.	3, 31, 43, 48
'Royal Sunset' (1960) Large-flowered climber, 8.1	Apricot fading to peach	4 1/2" double; slight scent; hybrid tealike buds; good bloom all season.	Glossy, broad, coppery green; vigorous grower to 10'; disease resistant; good on posts, fences, or small structures.	5, 38
'Climbing Shot Silk' (1931) Climbing hybrid tea, 7.8	Cherry cerise shading to golden yellow at base	Large semidouble; very fragrant; good flower production on long stems.	Dark, glossy; moderately vigorous to 15'; one of the hardiest climbing hybrid teas.	11, 37
'Sombreuil' (1850) Tea, 8.6	Ivory white	4" very double; strong tea fragrance; hundreds of furled petals; many blooms.	Light green, glossy; moderately vigorous to 8'–10'; tender; pendulous bloom; good on arbors, as best viewed from below.	13, 22, 33, 37
'Viking Queen' (1963) Large-flowered climber, 7.5	Medium to deep pink	3"–4" double; heavy fragrance; continual bloom.	Dark, glossy, leathery; grows to 12'–15'; hardy.	7, 10, 13, 33
'White Dawn' (1949) Large-flowered climber, 7.3	Pure white	2"–3" double; fragrant; gardenialike flowers in clusters; continual bloom but best displays in spring and fall.	Dark, glossy; vigorous growth to 10'–12'; disease resistant; quite hardy.	1, 2, 4, 10, 14, 15, 25, 29, 37, 40, 41, 48

'Cinderella'

'Foxy Lady'

Top: 'Gold Coin'
Above: 'Green Ice'

MINIATURE ROSES

Rose, year of introduction, awards, and ARS rating	Flower color	Flower description and blooming habits	Foliage, growth habits, and cultural tips	Catalog sources
'Baby Darling' (1964), 8.5	Orange to orange pink	1 3/4" double; slight fragrance.	Medium green; moderately compact, 12"–14"; relatively tender.	21, 24, 26, 28, 34, 36, 46
'Beauty Secret' (1965) ARS Award of Excellence 1975, 9.3	Cardinal red	1"–1 1/2" semidouble; very fragrant; hybrid tealike buds; abundant bloom; good cut.	Glossy, leathery; moderately compact, 8"–10"; very hardy; good in semishade.	9, 24, 26, 28, 30, 34, 35, 36, 39, 46
'Chattem Centennial' (1979), 8.0	Red	1 3/4" double; fragrant.	Glossy; compact.	9, 24, 26, 30, 35, 36, 46
'Choo Choo Centennial' (1980)	Pink	1 1/4" double; globular bud.	Glossy; moderately compact; disease resistant.	9, 24, 26, 36
'Cinderella' (1953), 8.7	White with pale pink edging	3/4"–1" double; spicy fragrance; white fading to pink; prolific; good cut.	Glossy; compact plant to 12"–15"; thornless; disease resistant; easy to grow; excellent in pots.	9, 16, 18, 21, 24, 26, 28, 34, 36
'Crazy Quilt' (1980)	Red and white	1" double; globular buds.	Glossy; compact.	24, 26, 28, 34, 39, 46
'Cupcake' (1981) ARS Award of Excellence	Pink	1 1/2" double; well-formed hybrid tealike buds; profuse bloomer.	Dark green; compact.	9, 26, 27, 28, 30, 35, 36, 46, 48
'Dreamglo' (1978), 8.0	Red and white blend	1 1/2" double; long, pointed hybrid tealike buds; long lasting.	Glossy; moderately compact; vigorous, healthy.	9, 24, 26, 27, 28, 30, 35, 36, 46
'Dwarfking' (1957) ('Zwergkönig'), 7.5	Rich dark red	3/4"–1" double; slight fragrance; hybrid tealike buds.	Glossy; moderately compact, 8"–10"; hardy; disease resistant.	24, 26
'Foxy Lady' (1980) 7.5	Coral pink to white blend	1 3/4" double; slight scent; singly or in clusters; profuse bloom.	Rich green; moderately compact, to 18".	1, 24, 26, 46
'Gold Coin' (1967), 7.5	Buttercup yellow	1 1/2" double; moderate fragrance; good color retention; hybrid tealike buds; abundant bloom.	Dark, leathery; low growing, very compact.	3, 9, 16, 18, 24, 26, 28, 36, 39

Top: 'Lavender Jewel'
Above: 'Holy Toledo'

'Judy Fischer'

'Lavender Lace'

Rose, year of introduction, awards, and ARS rating	Flower color	Flower description and blooming habits	Foliage, growth habits, and cultural tips	Catalog sources
'Green Ice' (1971), 7.9	White to soft green	1 1/2″ double; no scent; ivory white in sun, chartreuse in shade; profuse bloom in clusters; good cut.	Glossy, leathery, medium green; vigorous grower, short and spreading; disease resistant; likes some shade; easy to grow; good in hanging baskets.	8, 9, 15, 18, 21, 24, 26, 27, 28, 30, 34, 35, 36, 48
'Holy Toledo' (1978) ARS Award of Excellence 1980, 8.5	Apricot orange with yellow orange center and reverse	2″ double; slight fragrance; prolific, long-lasting blooms.	Deep green; glossy; vigorous, large grower to 20″.	24, 26, 27, 28, 30, 34, 36, 46
'Hula Girl' (1975), 7.7	Orange blend	1 1/2″ double; fruity fragrance, hybrid tealike buds; stable color.	Dark green; moderately compact to 10″; disease resistant.	8, 24, 26, 28, 34
'Judy Fischer' (1968) ARS Award of Excellence 1975, 8.8	Rose pink	1 1/2″ double; no fragrance; well-formed hybrid tealike buds; excellent color retention; good cut.	Bronzy, dark, leathery; moderately compact, bushy.	9, 21, 24, 26, 28, 30, 35, 36, 39, . 46
'Lavender Jewel' (1978), 8.0	Lavender mauve	1 1/2″ double; little fragrance; true color; many blooms over a long season; good cut.	Dark green, glossy; vigorous, moderately compact; disease resistant.	9, 15, 24, 26, 27, 28, 30, 34, 35, 36, 39, 41, 46
'Lavender Lace' (1968) ARS Award of Excellence 1975, 7.8	Lavender	1 1/2″ double; moderate fragrance; free blooming; long lasting; good cut.	Small, glossy; moderately compact, low and spreading; vigorous; disease resistant; good for growing under lights.	8, 9, 24, 26, 28, 34, 39, 46
'Luvvie' (1980)	Deep coral pink	5/8″–1″ double, a micromini; no fragrance; hybrid tealike buds; long lasting.	Deep green; a compact grower to 8″–12″; excellent container plant.	26, 35, 46
'Mary Marshall' (1970) ARS Award of Excellence 1975, 8.7	Orange with yellow base	1 3/4″ double; moderate fragrance; profuse bloom all season; good cut.	Leathery, medium green; moderately compact, 10″ –12″; disease resistant.	9, 24, 26, 28, 30, 34, 36, 39, 46

Top: 'Over the Rainbow'
Above: 'Puppy Love'

Top left: 'My Valentine'
Above: 'Starina'

Top right: 'Yellow Doll'

MINIATURE ROSES

Rose, year of introduction, awards, and ARS rating	Flower color	Flower description and blooming habits	Foliage, growth habits, and cultural tips	Catalog sources
'My Valentine' (1975), 7.7	Dark red	1 1/4″ double; no fragrance; long-lasting blooms.	Bronzy, glossy; moderately compact, 12″–14″; disease resistant; good for containers.	24, 26, 28, 34, 36, 39
'Orange Honey' (1979), 8.0	Orange yellow	1 1/2″ double; no fragrance; changing to different shades of orange and red while opening; free blooming.	Medium green; large, spreading shrub to 24″.	9, 15, 24, 26, 28, 34, 35, 36, 39, 41, 46
'Over the Rainbow' (1972) ARS Award of Excellence 1975, 8.5	Red and yellow	1 3/4″ double; little fragrance; abundant bloom; color stable.	Leathery, medium green; vigorous, bushy to 12″ –14″; disease resistant.	9, 24, 26, 28, 34, 35, 36, 39, 46
'Puppy Love' (1978) ARS Award of Excellence 1979, 8.0	Orange, pink, and coral blend	1 1/2″–1 3/4″ double; slight fragrance; borne singly on long stems; free blooming; good cut.	Glossy, small; compact, shapely to 16″; good in containers.	9, 24, 26, 28, 30, 35, 36, 48
'Rise 'n Shine' (1977) ARS Award of Excellence 1978, 8.5	Medium yellow	2″–2 1/4″ double; little fragrance; abundant and continuous bloom; good cut.	Small, glossy, deep green, good foil for the blossoms; moderately compact, vigorous to 12″–14″; disease resistant; easy to grow.	9, 15, 24, 26, 27, 28, 30, 34, 35, 36, 39, 41, 46, 48
'Snow Bride' (1982) ARS Award of Excellence 1983	White	1 3/4″ single; little fragrance; hybrid tealike buds.	Glossy; moderately compact.	9, 26, 27, 35, 36, 46
'Starina' (1965), 9.4	Orange scarlet	1 1/2″–2″ double, no fragrance; outstanding bud and flower form; abundant, continuous bloom; good cut.	Small, glossy; vigorous, moderately compact to 15″ –18″; relatively tender; top ARS rating of 9.4.	16, 24, 26, 27, 28, 30, 34, 36, 39, 46, 48
'White Angel' (1971) ARS Award of Excellence 1975, 8.4	White	1 1/4″ double; slight scent; hybrid tealike buds; profuse bloom.	Small, light green; moderately compact, 8″ –12″; nearly thornless.	24, 26, 28, 34, 39, 46
'Yellow Doll' (1962), 8.4	Yellow to cream	1 3/4″ double; moderate fragrance; free blooming.	Dark green, glossy, leathery; vigorous, moderately compact to 14″.	24, 26, 28, 30, 34, 35, 39, 46

ROSES FOR SPECIAL PURPOSES

All of the roses on the following lists have an American Rose Society rating of 6.0 or higher. (For an explanation of the rating system, see page 27.) The lists will give you an idea of the height, best use, or color of each variety. For more information on specific roses, see the "Encyclopedia of Roses."

KEY TO ABBREVIATIONS

A	Alba
B	Bourbon
C	Centifolia
Ch	China
Cl	Climbing
D	Damask
F	Floribunda
G	Gallica
Gr	Grandiflora
HP	Hybrid perpetual
HT	Hybrid tea
LCl	Large-flowered climber
M	Moss
Min	Miniature
N	Noisette
P	Portland
Pol	Polyantha
R	Rambler
S	Shrub
T	Tea

ROSES FOR TALL HEDGES AND SCREENS

Resist the temptation to plant roses too close together to form a hedge. Depending on their size when mature, the plants should be placed 3–5 feet apart to allow good air circulation and room for the plants to grow. All the following roses make fine hedges or screens.

'Buccaneer' (Gr)
'Complicata' (S)
'Eye Paint' (F)
'Great Maiden's Blush' (A)
'Medallion' (HT)
'Nevada' (S)
'Proud Land' (HT)
Rosa rugosa hybrids

ROSES FOR LOW HEDGES

Not surprisingly, the low-growing floribunda and polyantha roses dominate the selections in this landscaping category. Space the plants 2–3 feet apart for best results.

'Betty Prior' (F)
'Charisma' (F)
'Frau Dagmar Hastrup' (S)
'Garnette' (F)
'Ginger' (F)
'Happy' (Pol)
'Margo Koster' (Pol)
'Orangeade' (F)
'Perle d'Or' (Pol)
'Redgold' (F)
'The Fairy' (Pol)

ROSES FOR LOW EDGINGS

Miniature roses are perfect for use as an edging alongside a path or to mark the edge of a flower bed. The following cultivars are particularly good choices because of their compact habit. Allow 12–18 inches between each plant.

'Chattem Centennial'
'Cinderella'
'Crazy Quilt'
'Cupcake'
'Gold Coin'
'Judy Fischer'
'Luvvie'
'My Valentine'
'Starina'

ROSES FOR GROUND COVERS

Species hybrids and ramblers will generally sprawl over an area with little difficulty and no assistance on the part of the gardener, but climbers will need to be pegged down to train their growth horizontally. The following roses are all good candidates for use as ground covers.

'Félicité et Perpétue'
   (*R. sempervirens*, sport)
'New Dawn' (LCl)
Rosa laevigata
Rosa wichuraiana
   and its hybrids

'Oklahoma'

ROSES BY COLOR
RED ROSES

Species and Shrub Roses
'Cerise Bouquet'
Rosa moyesii
Rosa rugosa

Old Garden Roses
'Général Jacqueminot' (HP)
Rosa gallica officinalis (G)
'Tuscany Superb' (G)

Hybrid Tea Roses
'Arkansas'
'Big Ben'
'Charlotte Armstrong'
'Christian Dior'
'Chrysler Imperial'
'Crimson Glory'
'Fragrant Cloud'
'Futura'
'Mister Lincoln'
'National Trust'
'Oklahoma'
'Papa Meilland'
'Proud Land'
'Red Devil'
'Red Masterpiece'
'Rubaiyat'
'Swarthmore'

Floribunda and Polyantha Roses
'City of Belfast'
'Europeana'
'Eye Paint'
'Garnette'
'Happy'

Grandiflora Roses
'John S. Armstrong'
'Scarlet Knight'

Climbers, Ramblers, and Pillar Roses
'Altissimo'
'Blaze'
'Climbing Crimson Glory'
'Don Juan'
'Dortmund'
'Paul's Scarlet Climber'

Miniature Roses
'Beauty Secret'
'Chatten Centennial'
'Dwarfking'
'My Valentine'

'La Reine Victoria'

PINK ROSES

Species and Shrub Roses
'Complicata'
'Constance Spry'
'Frau Dagmar Hastrup'
'Pink Grootendorst'
Rosa eglanteria
Rosa rubrifolia
Rosa virginiana
'Stanwell Perpetual'

Old Garden Roses
'Baronne Prévost' (HP)
'Célestial' (A)
'Communis' (M)
'Comte de Chambord' (P)
'Crested Moss' (C)
'Duchesse de Brabant' (T)
'Fantin-Latour' (C)
'Great Maiden's Blush' (A)
'Hermosa' (Ch)
'Königin von Dänemark' (A)
'La Reine Victoria' (B)
'Maman Cochet' (T)
'Old Blush' (Ch)
Rosa centifolia bullata (C)
Rosa centifolia cristata (M)
Rosa centifolia pomponia (C)
Rosa damascena semperflorens (D)
Rosa damascena versicolor (D)
'Salet' (M)
'Souvenir de la Malmaison' (B)

Hybrid Tea Roses
'Bewitched'
'Dainty Bess'
'Duet'
'Electron'
'First Love'
'Friendship'
'La France'
'Michèle Meilland'
'Miss All-American Beauty'
'Perfume Delight'
'Peter Frankenfeld'
'Pink Favorite'
'Royal Highness'
'South Seas'
'Sweet Surrender'
'Tiffany'

Floribunda and Polyantha Roses
'Betty Prior'
'Cécile Brunner'
'Cherish'
'China Doll'
'Fashion'
'Gene Boerner'
'The Fairy'

Grandiflora Roses
'Aquarius'
'Camelot'
'Pink Parfait'
'Queen Elizabeth'
'Sonia'

Climbers, Ramblers, and Pillar Roses
'America'
'Climbing Cécile Brunner'
'Dr. W. Van Fleet'
'Kathleen'
'New Dawn'
'Rhonda'
'Viking Queen'

Miniature Roses
'Choo Choo Centennial'
'Cupcake'
'Judy Fischer'
'Luvvie'

ORANGE TO GOLD ROSES

Hybrid Tea Roses
'Antigua'
'Autumn Gold'
'Bing Crosby'
'Brandy'
'Command Performance'
'Medallion'
'Seashell'
'Sutter's Gold'
'Tropicana'
'Yankee Doodle'

Floribunda and Polyantha Roses
'Bahia'
'Cathedral'
'First Edition'
'Ginger'
'Margo Koster'
'Marina'
'Orangeade'
'Spartan'

Grandiflora Roses
'Arizona'
'Olé'
'Prominent'
'Shreveport'
'Sundowner'

Climbers, Ramblers, and Pillar Roses
'Climbing Baby Darling'
'Royal Sunset'

Miniature Roses
'Baby Darling'
'Holy Toledo'
'Hula Girl'
'Mary Marshall'
'Orange Honey'
'Starina'

YELLOW ROSES

Species and Shrub Roses
'Buff Beauty'
'Frühlingsgold'
'Golden Wings'
Rosa foetida persiana
Rosa harisonii
Rosa hugonis

Hybrid Tea Roses
'Irish Gold'
'King's Ransom'
'Oregold'
'Summer Sunshine'

Florinbunda and Polyantha Roses
'Perle d'Or'
'Sun Flare'

Grandiflora Roses
'Buccaneer'
'Gold Medal'

Climbers, Ramblers, and Pillar Roses
'Elegance'
'Golden Showers'
'Mermaid'

Miniature Roses
'Gold Coin'
'Rise 'n Shine'

WHITE TO CREAM ROSES

Species and Shrub Roses
'Blanc Double de Coubert'
'Nevada'
Rosa laevigata
Rosa wichuraiana
'Schneezwerg'

Old Garden Roses
'Lamarque' (N)
'Madame Hardy' (D)

Hybrid Tea Roses
'Garden Party'
'Honor'
'Pascali'
'Pristine'
'White Masterpiece'

Floribunda and Polyantha Roses
'French Lace'
'Iceberg'
'Ivory Fashion'

Grandiflora Roses
'Mount Shasta'
'White Lightnin' '

Climbers, Ramblers, and Pillar Roses
'Félicité et Perpétue'
'Sombreuil'
'White Dawn'

Miniature Roses
'Green Ice'
'Snow Bride'
'White Angel'
'Yellow Doll'

LAVENDER ROSES

Hybrid Tea Roses
'Blue Moon'
'Heirloom'
'Lady X'
'Paradise'
'Sterling Silver'

Floribunda Roses
'Angel Face'

Miniature Roses
'Lavender Jewel'
'Lavender Lace'

BICOLOR AND MULTICOLOR ROSES

Species and Shrub Roses
Rosa foetida bicolor

Old Garden Roses
'Ferdinand Pichard' (HP)
'Honorine de Brabant'
Rosa gallica versicolor (G)

Hybrid Tea Roses
'American Heritage'
'Chicago Peace'
'Color Magic'
'Confidence'
'Double Delight'
'First Prize'
'Granada'
'Helen Traubel'
'Kordes' Perfecta'
'Michèle Meilland'
'Mon Cheri'
'Neue Revue'
'Peace'
'Rose Gaujard'
'Spellbinder'
'Sutter's Gold'
'Yankee Doodle'

Floribunda and Polyantha Roses
'Charisma'
'Redgold'

Grandiflora Roses
'Cherry-Vanilla'
'Love'

Climbers, Ramblers, and Pillar Roses
'Handel'
'Joseph's Coat'
'Climbing Shot Silk'

Miniature Roses
'Cinderella'
'Crazy Quilt'
'Dreamglo'
'Fairlane'
'Over the Rainbow'
'Puppy Love'

EASIEST-TO-GROW ROSES

Few roses are difficult to grow, but the following cultivars are particularly easy to grow because of their high resistance to disease and vigorous growth. They will all perform well with a modicum of care.
'America' (LC1)
'Bewitched' (HT)
'Blaze' (LC1)
'Charlotte Armstrong' (HT)
'Cinderella' (Min)
'Europeana' (F)
'Fragrant Cloud' (HT)
'Futura' (HT)
'Green Ice' (Min)
'Mister Lincoln' (HT)
'Pink Parfait' (Gr)
'Queen Elizabeth' (Gr)
'Rise 'n Shine' (Min)
'Shreveport' (Gr)
'The Fairy' (Pol)

FRAGRANT ROSES

In the opinion of many gardeners, fragrance is one of the delightful attributes that, combined with flower form and color, make growing roses a special treat. If fragrance is also a prerequisite for you in choosing a rose, you'll want to consider the following roses. Roses marked with an asterisk (*) are remarkably fragrant.

Species Roses
Rosa eglanteria (Sweetbriar rose), fragrant foliage
Rosa laevigata (Cherokee rose)
Rosa rugosa

Shrub Roses
All shrub roses listed in the encyclopedia (page 64) are fragrant except 'Complicata', 'Golden Wings', 'Nevada', and 'Pink Grootendorst'.

Old Garden Roses
All the old garden roses listed in the encyclopedia (pages 66 and 69) are fragrant to some degree, but the following have an exceptional or heavy scent.
*'Communis' (M)
'Duchesse de Brabant' (T)
'Général Jacqueminot' (HP)
'Honorine de Brabant' (B)
'Königin von Dänemark' (A)
'Madame Hardy' (D)
Rosa centifolia bullata (C)
Rosa centifolia pomponi (C)
Rosa damascena semperflorens (D)
Rosa gallica officinalis (G)
'Salet' (M)

Hybrid Tea Roses
Hybrid tea roses that are winners of the James Alexander Gamble Rose Fragrance Medal (see page 27) are indicated by a dagger (†).
'Bewitched'
'Blue Moon'
'Candy Stripe'
†'Chrysler Imperial'
'Confidence'
†'Crimson Glory'
'Double Delight'
†'Fragrant Cloud'
†'Granada'
'Helen Traubel'
'Mister Lincoln'
'Oklahoma'
†'Papa Meilland'
'Perfume Delight'
'Proud Land'
'Rubaiyat'
'Seashell'
†'Sutter's Gold'
'Sweet Surrender'
†'Tiffany'

Floribunda Roses
*'Angel Face'
'Iceberg'
*'Spartan'

Grandiflora Roses
'Arizona'
'Sonia'
'Sundowner'
*'White Lightnin' '

Climbers, Ramblers, and Pillar Roses
*'Climbing Crimson Glory'
'Don Juan'
*'Climbing Shot Silk'
'Sombreuil'
'Viking Queen'

Miniature Roses
*'Beauty Secret'

'Fragrant Cloud'

'Angel Face'

'Paradise'

LONG-LASTING CUT ROSES

The following roses are particularly fine for cutting for indoor arrangements and will keep well for quite a few days, especially if you treat them as described on pages 55–56.

Hybrid Tea Roses
'Blue Moon'
'Charlotte Armstrong'
'Chicago Peace'
'Christian Dior'
'Chrysler Imperial'
'Double Delight'
'Duet'
'First Prize'
'Fragrant Cloud'
'Friendship'
'Futura'
'Garden Party'
'Honor'
'Medallion'
'Michèle Meilland'
'Miss All-American Beauty'
'Oklahoma'
'Paradise'
'Pascali'
'Peace'
'Perfume Delight'
'Peter Frankenfeld'
'Pink Favorite'
'Red Masterpiece'
'Royal Highness'
'Swarthmore'
'Tiffany'
'Tropicana'
'White Masterpiece'

Floribunda and Polyantha Roses
'Angel Face'
'Cathedral'
'Cécile Brunner'
'Charisma'
'Cherish'
'Europeana'
'First Edition'
'Marina'
Orangeade'

Grandiflora Roses
'Aquarius'
'Arizona'
'Love'
'Mount Shasta'
'Olé'
'Pink Parfait'
'Prominent'
'Queen Elizabeth'
'Scarlet Knight'
'Sonia'
'White Lightnin' '

Climbers, Ramblers, and Pillar Roses
'Climbing Crimson Glory'
'Don Juan'
'Rhonda'

Miniature Roses
'Beauty Secret'
'Cinderella'
'Golden Angel'
'Green Ice'
'Judy Fischer'
'Lavender Jewel'
'Lavender Lace'
'Mary Marshall'
'Puppy Love'
'Rise 'n Shine'
'Starina'

HARDIEST ROSES

Few modern roses can withstand sustained winter temperatures below 10°F, so providing them with some sort of winter protection in cold-winter climates is almost mandatory. The roses listed below should still have some protection in northern climates, but they have shown great resilience under harsh conditions.
'Bewitched' (HT)
'Blue Moon' (HT)
'Christian Dior' (HT)
'Crimson Glory' (HT)
'Europeana' (F)
'Fragrant Cloud' (HT)
'Garden Party' (HT)
'Lady X' (HT)
'Pink Parfait' (Gr)
'Pristine' (HT)
'Rubaiyat' (HT)
'Swarthmore' (HT)

MOST DISEASE-RESISTANT ROSES

We can't guarantee that all of the roses listed below will be completely immune to diseases, but with a small amount of preventive maintenance and early-season spraying or dusting, these sturdy plants are likely to remain healthy.
'Confidence' (HT)
'First Prize' (HT)
'Fragrant Cloud' (HT)
'Pink Parfait' (Gr)
'Pristine' (HT)
'Rubaiyat' (HT)
'Shreveport' (Gr)

CATALOG SOURCES

The following list will tell you which rose growers and nurseries specialize in certain kinds of roses, and which are generalists. The list is keyed to the last column in the charts, "Catalog Sources." The information on suppliers was correct at the time of publication, but because varieties carried by mail-order suppliers vary from year to year, you should write for a catalog or list before ordering. Supplies are often limited, so order early. It's always a good idea to list alternate selections in case the variety you want is out of stock.

ROSE SUPPLIERS

Armstrong Nurseries Inc. (1)
P.O. Box 4060
Ontario, CA 91761
A major developer of roses and fruit trees. Free colorful catalog.

Buckley Nursery Company (2)
646 North River Road
Buckley, WA 98321
List of modern roses, including tree roses.

W. Atlee Burpee Co. (3)
300 Park Avenue
Warminster, PA 18974
Free, color spring catalog lists popular new rose varieties and some old favorites among a wide selection of garden plants and seeds.

Carroll Gardens (4)
Box 310
Westminster, MD 21157
Catalog $1.00, refundable with first order; lists perennials, trees, and shrubs with many modern roses.

Roses by Fred Edmunds, Inc. (5)
6235 S.W. Kahle Road
Wilsonville, OR 97070
Free color catalog lists a wide variety of modern roses.

Emlong Nurseries Inc. (6)
Box #ROSES
Stevensville, MI 49127
Free garden catalog includes a selection of modern roses.

Farmer Seed & Nursery Company (7)
818 N.W. 4th Street
Fairbault, MN 55021
Free color catalog includes a small selection of roses, including many winter-hardy varieties.

Henry Field Seed & Nursery Co. (8)
407 Sycamore Street
Shenandoah, IA 51602
Free color catalogs in spring and fall offer a limited number of modern roses.

Gloria Dei Nursery (9)
36 East Road
High Falls Park
High Falls, NY 12440
Specializes in miniatures; free catalog.

Gurney Seed and Nursery (10)
Gurney Building
Yankton, SD 57078
Free color catalog includes many new and old rose varieties.

Heritage Rose Gardens (11)
16831 Mitchell Creek Drive
Fort Bragg, CA 95437
Free listing of a wide selection of species, shrub, and old roses.

High Country Rosarium (12)
1717 Downing Street
Denver, CO 80218
Catalog $1.00; specializing in hardy old species and shrub roses.

Historical Roses (13)
1657 West Jackson Street
Painesville, OH 44077
Free listing of shrub and old roses with some popular modern and climbing roses.

Hortico (14)
RR 1 Robson Road
Waterdown, Ontario
Canada L0R 2H0
Free list of a good selection of modern roses.

Inter-State Nurseries, Inc. (15)
504 E Street
Hamburg, IA 51640
Spring and fall catalogs include a wide selection of roses. Gardens open 7 days a week.

Jackson & Perkins Company (16)
1 Rose Lane
Medford, OR 97501
Free 40-page color catalog of modern roses, plus fruit trees and bulbs.

J.W. Jung Seed Company (17)
Randolph, WI 53956
Free color catalog offers a selection of popular modern roses.

Kelly Brothers Nursery Inc. (18)
Dansville, NY 14437
Free color catalog. Limited selection of modern and shrub roses.

Joseph J. Kern Nursery (19)
Box 33
Mentor, OH 44060
Free list primarily of old roses, all in very limited supply.

Krider Nurseries Inc. (20)
P.O. Box 29
Middlebury, IN 46540
Free catalog offers a good selection of roses.

Lamb Nurseries (21)
E. 101 Sharp Avenue
Spokane, WA 99202
Free catalog includes hardy miniature roses.

Liggett's Rose Nursery (22)
1206 Curtiff Avenue
San Jose, CA 95125
Free list of classic modern and old roses, many in short supply.

Lyndon Lyon Greenhouses, Inc. (23)
14 Mutchler Street
Dolgeville, NY 13329
Specialists in hybridizing miniature roses and exotic house plants. Color catalog $.50; offers some miniature roses among other exotic houseplants.

McDaniel's Miniature Roses (24)
7523 Zemco Street
Lemon Grove, CA 92045
Free list of miniature varieties.

Earl May Seed & Nursery Company (25)
Shenandoah, IA 51603
Sub-zero roses and modern classifications; also products for growers. Free color catalog includes a selection of modern roses.

Miniature Plant Kingdom (26)
4125 Harrison Grade Road
Sebastopol, CA 95472
Catalog $1.00, refundable; lists over 500 varieties of miniature roses.

The Miniature Rose Company (27)
200 Rose Ridge
Greenwood, SC 29647
Free color catalog offers a large selection of miniatures.

Mini-Roses (28)
P.O. Box 4255, Station A
Dallas, TX 75208
Free list of miniature roses.

Neosho Nurseries (29)
P.O. Box 550
Neosho, MO 64850
Free color catalog offers a good selection of favorite modern roses.

Nor'East Miniature Roses (30)
58 Hammond Street
Rowley, MA 01969
Free color catalog of a wide variety of miniature roses.

Carl Pallek and Sons Nurseries (31)
Box 137
Virgil, Ontario
Canada L0S 1T0
Free list of modern roses. Will ship to Canadian customers only. Hard-to-find roses, including some shrubs.

Perry Roses (32)
1201 Pineview Drive
Raleigh, NC 27606
Free list of personally-hybridized hybrid tea roses.

Pickering Nursery (33)
670 Kingston Road
Pickering, Ontario
Canada L1V 1A6
Free extensive list of a wide range of modern, shrub, and old roses.

Pixie Treasures (34)
4121 Prospect Avenue
Yorba Linda, CA 92686
Free list of a large selection of miniature roses. Visitors welcome.

Redlyn Nursery (35)
Route 2, Box 144-B
Umatilla, FL 32784
Free brochure lists a good selection of miniature roses.

Rosehill Farm (36)
Box 406
Greg Neck Road
Galena, MD 21635
Free list of a fine selection of miniature roses.

Roses of Yesterday and Today (37)
802 Brown's Valley Road
Watsonville, CA 95076
Catalog $2.00; offers an extensive selection of old and rare roses plus a few modern roses.

Roseway Nursery (38)
8766 N.E. Sandy Boulevard
Portland, OR 97220
Free color catalog of modern varieties.

Sequoia Nursery (39)
Moore Miniature Roses
2519 E. Noble Avenue
Visalia, CA 93277
Free catalog lists a large selection of miniature roses by one of the top hybridizers.

Spring Hill Nurseries Co., Inc. (40)
6523 N. Galena Road
Peoria, IL 61632
Free color catalog offers an extensive selection of modern roses.

Stanek's Nursery (41)
2929 27th Avenue
Spokane, WA 99203
Modern cultivars, supplies, and some shrub roses. Free color catalog of a good selection of modern roses.

Stark Bros. Nurseries (42)
Box 1196-C
Louisiana, MO 63393
A small selection of modern roses in a free color catalog.

C. H. Stocking Nursery (43)
785 N. Capitol Avenue
San Jose, CA 95133
Catalog lists modern cultivars, miniatures, and some novelty roses. Free color catalog of an extensive selection of modern roses.

Tate Nursery (44)
Route 20, Box 436
Tyler, TX 75708
Free list of a good selection of modern roses.

Thomasville Nurseries, Inc. (45)
P.O. Box 7
Thomasville, GA 31792
Free listing of a good selection of modern roses.

Tiny Petals Miniature Roses (46)
489 Minot Avenue
Chula Vista, CA 92010
Free listing of a wide selection of miniature roses.

Van Bourgondien Brothers (47)
P.O. Box A
245 Farmingdale Road
Babylon, NY 11702
Free color garden catalog includes a few hedge roses.

Wayside Gardens (48)
Hodges, SC 29695
Color catalog includes listing of wide variety of modern roses.

INDEX

NOTE: Italicized page numbers refer to illustrations.

U.S. Measure and Metric Measure Conversion Chart

Formulas for Exact Measures

Rounded Measures for Quick Reference

	Symbol	When you know:	Multiply by:	To find:			
Mass	oz	ounces	28.35	grams	1 oz		= 30 g
(Weight)	lb	pounds	0.45	kilograms	4 oz		= 115 g
	g	grams	0.035	ounces	8 oz		= 225 g
	kg	kilograms	2.2	pounds	16 oz	= 1 lb	= 450 g
					32 oz	= 2 lb	= 900 kg
					36 oz	= 2-1/4 lb	= 1000 g (1 kg)
Volume	tsp	teaspoons	5.0	milliliters	1/4 tsp	= 1/24 oz	= 1 ml
	tbsp	tablespoons	15.0	milliliters	1/2 tsp	= 1/12 oz	= 2 ml
	fl oz	fluid ounces	29.57	milliliters	1 tsp	= 1/6 oz	= 5 ml
	c	cups	0.24	liters	1 tbsp	= 1/2 oz	= 15 ml
	pt	pints	0.47	liters	1 c	= 8 oz	= 250 ml
	qt	quarts	0.95	liters	2 c (1 pt)	= 16 oz	= 500 ml
	gal	gallons	3.785	liters	4 c (1 qt)	= 32 oz	= 1 l
	ml	milliliters	0.034	fluid ounces	4 qt (1 gal)	= 128 oz	= 3-3/4 l
Length	in.	inches	2.54	centimeters	3/8 in.	= 1 cm	
	ft	feet	30.48	centimeters	1 in.	= 2.5 cm	
	yd	yards	0.9144	meters	2 in.	= 5 cm	
	mi	miles	1.609	kilometers	2-1/2 in.	= 6.5 cm	
	km	kilometers	0.621	miles	12 in. (1 ft)	= 30 cm	
	m	meters	1.094	yards	1 yd	= 90 cm	
	cm	centimeters	0.39	inches	100 ft	= 30 m	
					1 mi	= 1.6 km	
Temperature	°F	Fahrenheit	5/9 (after subtracting 32)	Celsius	32°F	= 0°C	
					68°F	= 20°C	
	°C	Celsius	9/5 (then add 32)	Fahrenheit	212°F	= 100°C	
Area	in.^{2}	square inches	6.452	square centimeters	1 in.^{2}	= 6.5 cm^2	
	ft^2	square feet	929.0	square centimeters	1 ft^2	= 930 cm^2	
	yd^2	square yards	8361.0	square centimeters	1 yd^2	= 8360 cm^2	
	a	acres	0.4047	hectares	1 a	= 4050 m^2	